Discovering the Naturalist Intelligence

Science in the School Yard

Jenna Glock, Maggie Meyer, and Susan Wertz

Zephyr Press

Tucson, Arizona

About Zephyr Press

Founded in 1979 in Tucson, Arizona, Zephyr Press continually strives to provide quality, innovative products for our customers, with the goal of improving learning opportunities for all children. With a focus on gifted education, multiple intelligences, and brain-compatible learning, Zephyr Press material is selected to help *all* children reach their highest potential.

Discovering the Naturalist Intelligence
Science in the School Yard

Grades: 1 through 6

© 1999 by Jenna Glock, Susan Wertz, and Maggie Meyer
Printed in the United States of America

ISBN 1-56976-089-6

Original illustrations by Catherine Conzatti
Editors: Veronica Durie and Stacey Shropshire
Cover design: Daniel Miedaner
Design and production: Daniel Miedaner

Published by:
Zephyr Press
P.O. Box 66006
Tucson, AZ 85728-6006
800-232-2187
www.zephyrpress.com
www.i-home-school.com

Library of Congress Cataloging-in-Publication Data

Glock, Jenna. 1967-
    Discovering the naturalist intelligence : science in the school
yard / Jenna Glock. Maggie Meyer, and Susan Wertz.
      p.   cm.
    Includes bibliographical references.
    ISBN 1-56976-089-6 (alk. paper)
    1. Science—Study and teaching—Activity programs. 2. Science
teachers—Training of. 3. Gardner, Howard. Multiple intelligence.
I. Meyer, Maggie (Margaret) 1947-   . II. Wertz, Susan, 1948-
III. Title.
Q181-G455 1999
372.3'5044—dc21   98-35959

Contents

Foreword

oward Gardner's theory of multiple intelligences has been enthusiastically received by so many educators because it speaks to their beliefs about the potential of children: teachers who use MI believe that all children have strengths, that all children *can* learn, and recognize that it is the job of the educator to use children's many intelligences in helping them learn. This book will be a powerful tool in teachers' palettes.

More than fifteen years ago Gardner set forth his initial proposition that multiple intelligences exist. At that time he said that if there were seven intelligences, it was reasonable to assume that more would be "found." A few years ago Gardner applied his rigorous criteria and identified an eighth intelligence: the naturalist. This book gives teachers many ways to bring the naturalist intelligence to life.

At first glance one might think that the naturalist intelligence has few implications for classroom teachers. After all, classrooms are almost always found within buildings and a naturalist setting is, by definition, outdoors. But as these authors show, this dichotomy need not be the case. The authors of this book have brought an incredible array of talent, creativity, and energy together to produce a work that will enable teachers to utilize the naturalist intelligence as one more tool to help their children grow. As the authors show in creative lesson plan after creative plan, some forms of observing, classifying and predicting, and problem solving with integral strategies can be done easily—and perhaps done best—in a naturalist setting. And there are some students who transform when they are allowed to use their naturalist intelligence; they become explorers, collectors, and experimenters. The recalcitrant student frequently becomes an active, inquisitive learner.

This book is very teacher friendly and pragmatic, from the use of the National Science Standards to the organization of the text around process skills and the Scientific Method to the listing of literature entry points for teachers' easy reference. Of particular note is the design of the lesson plans. They reflect teachers' needs, listing not just the applicable science standards and materials but offering curriculum extensions and strategies to check for understanding, as well as outlining reflection prompts.

One of the criticisms—unfounded but no less loud at times—of using multiple intelligence theory in schools is that doing so implies a backing away from standards and academic rigor. This book clearly shows the speciousness of that argument. Teachers who use these lessons will be teaching students to think critically, to solve problems, and to become learners.

Although it focuses on the naturalist intelligence, *Discovering the Naturalist Intelligence* does more than that. It also addresses each of the other intelligences. *Discovering the Naturalist Intelligence: Science in the School Yard* will be a valuable tool for teachers who already use the outdoors as a classroom as well as those (myself included) who think "roughing it" is a hotel room with a black and white TV. Enjoy!!

Thomas R. Hoerr, Ph.D.
Director, The New City School, St. Louis, Mo.

Preface

When Howard Gardner identified the naturalist intelligence, he confirmed something that the authors had known for years. Some people learn best when experiences are provided that take them outside into the natural world.

Elementary teachers don't specialize in just one discipline. They know a little about everything, but not everything about any one subject area. In this time of restructuring and change, expecting all teachers to be science specialists isn't realistic. In many cases, science has often been one of the disciplines K–6 teachers feel they are the least prepared to teach. Yet elementary teachers need to provide students' with learning opportunities that include observation skills, data collection methods, prediction, analysis, and communication of ideas. We designed this book so educators would feel comfortable putting their students in naturalist situations to develop science skills. We formatted this book so teachers would be able to easily interpret the background information and allow students to develop science process skills. We want teachers to find this book easy to implement and enjoyable to use. We hope that, when teachers feel successful using this book, they will push themselves to take a more in-depth approach to science.

Each lesson is based on the process skill listed, states a purpose, and reflects a National Science Standard. A segment is devoted to background information, which we have purposely kept short because elementary teachers need to have the flexibility of integrating these lessons into their current curriculum. We suggest a literature entry point and a connection that provides for emotional learning. We have constructed lesson procedures and data sheets for most lessons. We also make curriculum extension suggestions for those who want to do more.

We understand the importance of assessment and recognize that asking students to reflect on their experiences is one way to determine whether learning has taken place. For each lesson, we list ideas of ways to check for understanding. We also suggest and provide reflection prompts for the intrapersonal learner. We produced data sheets to help you prepare lessons and to use as ongoing assessment. Finally, we agree with Campbell, Dickinson, and Campbell (1992): "Assessing learning in natural contexts, in familiar environments, and with familiar tools and activities enables students to demonstrate their knowledge more effectively than through decontextualized, standardized approaches. The boundaries between assessment and instruction begin to dissolve when assessment occurs while students are actively engaged in usual classroom experiences" (199).

You can adapt or change all lessons to fit the needs and levels of various students. We know teachers are masters at adaptation. We encourage you to stretch and mold these lessons to make them your own. We hope this is a resource you will keep close to your desks to pull out when you want to address all the intelligences and not just the naturalist.

Acknowledgments

ecause teachers often work in isolation, several obstacles to sharing information seem to exist. Yet several people broke through those barriers to become for us models of communicating, motivating, inspiring, and sharing expertise.

To Tom Hoerr, director of The New City School in St. Louis—We met you at a multiple intelligence conference in Tucson, Arizona, in 1995. Your work and the work of the faculty at The New City School were a source of inspiration for us. We weren't confident we could put together this book while maintaining the demanding pace of teaching full time. The fact that you wrote two books on succeeding with MI encouraged us to give it a try. Through our e-mail relationship with you, you share opinions, thoughts, and information that directly affect our success. You have also become our head cheerleader. You not only believe all children can be successful, but firmly believe all teachers can succeed, also. You are an exemplary model for all school leaders today.

To Bill Stapp, Professor Emeritus at the University of Michigan—thank you for creating the very network that brought us all together. Without your vision, inspiration, ideas, and GREEN, we would have never discovered the true link among kids, nature, and our own communities. Yes, it is water that bonds us and caring that keeps us reaching out every day for new beginnings and answers for tomorrow.

To Rochelle Blackman Rothaus, coordinator of the South Sound Watershed Alliance—You support teachers in five different school districts and connect them to support systems in the community that enable them to provide watershed-based education for their students. (We are members of this group of teachers.) We have watched you work to exhaustion with a smile on your face and an offer to do more. Your attitude and support for our concepts and beliefs is definitely worth acknowledging.

To our families—This has been a very long endeavor. We truly could not have pulled this one off without your support and understanding through the many late nights and weekends we were absent—and to answer your unending question of "Is it done yet?" Yes—this one is!

Introduction

Reviewing the Seven Intelligences and Unwrapping the Eighth

Gardner (1993) defines *intelligence* as the "ability to solve problems or fashion products that are valued in one or more cultural or community settings." In his original work, he outlined seven intelligences. In 1995, he added the naturalist intelligence. Following is a brief description of these intelligences.

Verbal-linguistic:	the ability to recognize, understand, and compose meaning with words
Logical-mathematical:	the ability to learn through numbers, order, and reasoning
Visual-spatial:	the ability to conceive mental images and transform them
Musical-rhythmic:	the ability to learn, create, and communicate through rhythm, rhymes, and musical patterns
Bodily-kinesthetic:	the ability to learn by using simulations (becoming) and other highly physically skilled methods
Intrapersonal:	the ability to know the self
Interpersonal:	the ability to work with and understand others
Naturalist:	the ability to understand patterns, relationships, and connections in nature

Each intelligence is utilized to some degree in various ways by each person. All people are considered gifted and usually excel in one or two intelligences.

Gardner's perspective provides Western educators with a new concept of what is smart that looks beyond only mathematical and linguistic talent. No longer can we be content with providing only for these two intelligences. We must consider the variety of other ways in which kids learn and process information. All children can be successful if they are provided a variety of learning opportunities. Because the naturalist is the most recent of Gardner's discoveries and therefore has less information about using it in the classroom, we chose to focus on that intelligence while integrating it with other identified intelligences.

The Naturalist Intelligence

The sun shines not on us, but in us. The rivers flow not past, but through us.

—John Muir

Gardner defines a naturalist as a person who recognizes flora and fauna plus other consequential distinctions in the natural world and uses this ability productively. In our culture the term *naturalist* is applied to people who have an outstanding knowledge of the living world. Gardner mentions Charles Darwin and E. O. Wilson. Others are Sylvia Earle and Jane Goodall.

Naturalist Checklist

You can identify a child or adult who has a strong naturalist intelligence through observation. Usually a naturalist is a person who

- ❏ is very comfortable outdoors
- ❏ chooses to read books and watch programs about animals and the ecosystem
- ❏ nurtures living things (plants and animals)
- ❏ readily follows cyclic phenomena such as tides, seasons, phases of the moon, and climate
- ❏ recognizes patterns, colors, and classifications
- ❏ automatically uses senses to explore the environment
- ❏ observes patiently
- ❏ feels a definite connection and relationship with nature
- ❏ feels an affinity for natural habitats such as oceans, forests, deserts, and wetlands
- ❏ wants to view and appreciate the aesthetics of nature
- ❏ favors natural settings over the human-influenced environment
- ❏ is renewed by visiting natural settings
- ❏ is constantly aware of surroundings
- ❏ touches and explores "yucky things"
- ❏ enjoys collections of rocks, minerals, leaves, flowers, shells, feathers, and so on
- ❏ seeks music related to nature
- ❏ prefers to go to a zoo over an amusement park
- ❏ sets up feeding stations for birds, small mammals, and other wildlife
- ❏ participates in volunteer projects that benefit plants, animals, watersheds, or Earth
- ❏ uses binoculars, telescopes, microscopes, and hand lenses when observing
- ❏ feels satisfaction in learning names of flowers, trees, animals, rocks and minerals, cloud types, volcanoes, and so on
- ❏ collects articles, posters, pictures, figurines, stuffed animals that relate to wildlife or nature
- ❏ grows plants (gardens, window boxes, indoor plants, herbs)
- ❏ photographs or sketches animals, plants, habitats (places)
- ❏ shares observations with others (enjoys showing something such as a flower blooming or small insect)
- ❏ shows a sense for detail and notices even the smallest things
- ❏ manipulates equipment to find out more about environmental water test kits, butterfly nets, plant presses, and so on
- ❏ makes crafts and projects of natural materials (dried arrangements, plant presses, shells, and wood)
- ❏ documents by sketching, photographing, or listing natural phenomena
- ❏ names pet stores, aquariums, wild life parks, zoos, farms, and so on as "special places"
- ❏ enjoys recreations such as hiking, fishing, mountain or rock climbing, cross country skiing, camping, sailing, scuba diving, and so on

Educational Implications for the Naturalist Intelligence

Developing the naturalist intelligence is no less important than teaching math or reading skills. We must provide the opportunity for this intelligence to grow. Our primary responsibility is to be sure all children have a chance to experience success. We must consider all children and the skills they need to grow, all ways to deliver curriculum, all intelligences when planning and organizing lessons. As Tom Hoerr (1996) states, "The naturalist intelligence offers one more way to help students understand and learn" (xxiv). Successful employment in our students' future requires them to be computer literate, so we have stocked our classrooms and constructed computer labs to provide this opportunity. In a similar way, the quality of life on this planet requires that our children have some experience with nature. We must provide the best educational learning opportunities for this intelligence.

We are faced with determining the various benchmarks for learning and teaching to standards. Naturalist topics and themes integrate the curriculum in ways that will help us reach these goals. For example, change, cycles, and connections are themes that would help curriculum revolve around the ecosystem where the school is located. Teachers in the Pacific Northwest could develop integrated studies of marine ecology, watersheds, forests, and aquatic life. Educators in the Southwest could focus on the desert. Knowing and understanding your environment and using it as an extended classroom just makes sense.

But how do we develop such knowledge and understanding? How do we extend our classroom in such a way? Getting on a bus to go to an appropriate site is just as important as walking down the hall to the gym or the art room. Doing field studies allows one to see patterns in nature that are no different from the pattern blocks children use in math class. By observing outside, we can understand these connections.

Learning Strategies for the Naturalist

Provide opportunities that encourage the following:

- Observing through senses: feeling, smelling, listening
- Collecting data from observation
- Grouping natural objects (classification)
- Observing animal behavior
- Growing things—plants, gardens, butterfly garden
- Creating worm boxes and recycling projects
- Doing field studies out of doors
- Observing through the microscope, telescope, binoculars, hand lens
- Drawing, sketching, photographing, videotaping nature
- Manipulating outdoor equipment or kits (such as water testing kits or nets)
- Observing, reflecting, and journalizing silently outdoors
- Identifying sounds in nature
- Interacting with animals, bugs, and plants
- Establishing nature trails, viewing decks, or outdoor classrooms
- Inventing scientific instruments
- Designing experiments
- Going on real, electronic, video, and imagined field trips

- Walking outside in fresh air to listen to sounds of nature and feel dirt underfoot
- Modeling, measuring, or drawing to scale animals, plants, or outdoor settings
- Writing poems or songs using adjectives from the outdoors
- Identifying shapes in natural setting
- Observing plants or changes outdoors over the course of the school year
- Observing a fruit, vegetable, or other plant or animal material decompose over time
- Collecting trash or other items (rocks, feathers, flowers, leaves) in the school yard and grouping the items by their characteristics
- Reading aloud stories or articles that relate to the outdoors, space, natural phenomena, animals, and plants
- Performing role-plays of cycles in nature, animal behavior, plant growth, and so on

Process Skills Developed by Naturalist Learning Opportunities

A process skill is a basic tool in the world of learning and problem solving. The process skills needed to develop the naturalist intelligence are those that encourage exploration, discovery, creativity, and innovation. Most scientists would identify these skills as part of the scientific method. The logical progression of this method begins with observation of the world around us, which means simply stopping and taking in information through the senses when appropriate.

As the foundation of these experiences builds, the questions being to flow. Why does this happen? How did that work? The *whys* and *hows* can be answered through data collection, which is a way of recording the information: drawing, writing descriptions, and graphing to name a few. *Data collection* simply means that the experiences are not just consumed but measured in a way that can be remembered and later investigated. One can count on all sorts of estimating, measuring, counting, sorting, and classifying activities in this book.

Eventually, from the collected data, students can predict something or solve a problem to possibly answer the original question. On occasion the question goes unanswered because the students needs to observe more, collect more data, and predict and analyze further.

Following are brief definitions of the process skills used in this book. Many contain suggestions of activities that are appropriate to develop those skills.

- **Observing:** Using one or more of the five senses to gather information, often aided by the use of scientific equipment

- **Collecting data:** Gathering information through observation and measurement in a systematic manner
  - **Drawing and sketching:** Creating visual images of observations
  - **Describing:** Using words to record qualities
  - **Recording:** Documenting what has been observed
  - **Measuring:** Comparing objects to arbitrary units that may or may not be standardized

- **Predicting:** Forming an idea of an expected result based on inferences; guessing an outcome based on experience or evidence
  - **Estimating:** Calculating an approximate quantity or value based on judgment

- **Analyzing:** Looking at the data and trying to discover what it means
  - **Comparing:** Pointing out similarities of and differences between two or more things
  - **Classifying:** Grouping or ordering objects or events according to observed common characteristics
  - **Graphing:** Converting numerical quantities into a diagram that shows the relationship among them
  - **Calculating:** Adding things up
  - **Ordering:** Ranking, separating, or grouping

- **Communicating:** Giving or exchanging information orally or in writing to discover answers
  - **Cooperating:** Working together to share knowledge and create a better understanding
  - **Problem solving:** With the help of others, using observations, collected data, and analysis of information to draw conclusions or answer a question

Teaching for Understanding through Cross-Age Tutoring

Using the multiple intelligences as a tool to develop curriculum enhances understanding, which is the desired result of all schooling. Many times Maggie engages students in experiences but isn't confident that they understand what she hopes the experiences would lead them to understand. She often asks herself what she accomplished. She uses various forms of assessment to determine if learning has taken place. Her students have been involved in projects, presentations, teacher-made tests, student-made tests, student-designed rubrics, and portfolios that were used in student-led conferences. All these tools were helpful, but one of the more effective tools she used was cross-age tutoring with the lessons in this book as a foundation. Cross-age tutoring is a wonderful way to develop a true learning community.

An old Chinese proverb notes that people learn 10 percent of what they read, 20 percent of what they hear, 30 percent of what they see, 50 percent of what they see and hear, 70 percent of what they discuss with others, 80 percent of what they experience personally, and 95 percent of what they teach to someone else. During the school year Maggie involved her students in most of the lessons in this book. Students did some reading, but they mostly listened, looked, discussed, and personally experienced the natural environment that surrounds her school. Maggie's taught natural science to two first-grade classes in our building. The sixth graders experienced the lessons, mastered the objectives, then, every Friday afternoon, taught the lessons to the first graders. Not only was everyone involved in learning, but students developed leadership, responsibility, organization, integrity, and other life skills.

Everyone, teachers included, looked forward to Friday afternoon. Maggie's students valued these performances, finding them relevant and authentic. She engaged a variety of intelligences. She often adapted the lessons to the curriculum of the first graders and to her curriculum needs. She found the lessons in this book simple but adaptable for use with older students. She has also used this book in what she calls her *messing around stage*. She is looking forward to developing a thematic approach to these natural experiences so she can integrate the curriculum at higher levels.

Using the Outdoors for a Learning Environment

Our experiences have illustrated time and time again that effective learning is often heightened in a natural setting. Nature provides its own context—the living world and how we interact with it. The school yard or any other natural setting may enhance learning when it is incorporated into instruction. It seems increasingly important in this urbanized and technical age where information is often delivered abstractly or secondhand to ensure that students have a firsthand, meaningful experience with the natural world that surrounds them. It is such natural explorations and discoveries that lead students to understand and remember important concepts. Outdoor experiences provide foundational experiences that students embrace and carry throughout their lives. In our experiences, a student who has been grounded in the outdoors as a classroom is more apt to continue active learning past the formal school day in organizations such as Ecology Club, Stream Team, Junior Audubon Society, and Earth Service Corps.

Though nature is considered a topic for scientific study, environmental education is interdisciplinary. In each lesson, we give you examples of connections to language skills, literature, mathematics, social studies, and health. We don't ask you to use the lessons as add-ons. We urge you to use these studies as connectors and umbrellas for many of the skills and concepts that students need. By providing this experiential kind of learning, you help students pass from awareness to knowledge to understanding.

Using the outdoor environment as a natural classroom can take many forms. It can be as simple as looking out the window or actively using the school grounds as a setting for learning. If you choose the latter, you must consider several factors before taking your class outside. The initial extra work will be worth the effort as your students experience the connections between what they learn in school and the outdoor environment. The following information is meant to help you, not to block you. Taking students outdoors becomes easier the more experiences you and your students have.

Safety

Like any trip, a trip outside is not risk free. You should have training in first aid and CPR. Plan a procedure for notifying the office in case of an emergency and inform all students what that plan is. When far from the school office, always take a backpack that includes a small first aid kit, binoculars, extra clothes, water, and a cellular phone. Show pictures or maps of the route, site, and any hazards.

Know and warn students about plants and animals that may be dangerous. You can seek such advice from local experts (county extension agent, soil conservation service, master gardener, and so on) or publications. Students should not eat or taste any fruits, mushrooms, seeds, leaves, or anything else. Mushrooms especially can be deadly, and students should wash their hands after even touching any. Know whether there is any local poison ivy or poison oak (they are serious—much worse then nettles).

Most school yard critters can be examined and handled with no harm to the organism or the student. However, we would specify exactly what creatures the students are allowed to handle. Caution students to avoid dense underbrush and to avoid bees or wasps, and forbid them from reaching into holes. Some caterpillars' hair contains irritants to ward off predators and can irritate the skin, as well. Forbid students from contacting live or dead wild mammals, and instruct them to give wide range to any animal that is acting strangely, especially bats and raccoons. Bites and scratches from wild critters can carry tetanus and other potential dangers and should receive immediate professional medical attention. If students do need to collect, train them in handling specimens. Remind students to see you immediately if they get any cuts, bites, or scrapes.

Find out from your school nurse or parents if any students have health problems or allergies. Include the appropriate materials in your first-aid kit.

Notify your school office when you go outside. Establish boundaries of the study area. Tell your students that if they can't see you, they have wandered too far and should return immediately to a designated spot. Ultimately, it is your responsibility to keep them within your sight. You might want to use a bird whistle, duck call, or some other appropriate tool to get their attention if they wander too far.

Pair or team students, making each person responsible for keeping track of someone else during the trip. Pairs and cooperative groups are also essential for most data collection.

Practice good hygiene. After handling debris, outside plants, or soil wash your hands with soap or germicidal solution and rinse well.

When working with trash, use tongs to pick up broken glass, and deposit it in a bucket, not in a trash bag. Wear heavy garden gloves or, at the very least, rubber gloves when handling debris. Decide on a list of items that students must not collect, including specifically hospital wastes, such as hypodermic syringes or plasma bags; condoms; or tampon applicators. Some students may also be disturbed by picking up cigarette butts.

Behavior

Students need to understand that the outdoors is just an extension of the classroom. The same expectations you have in the classroom are rules outside, as well. Students can help develop and agree to rules for outside behavior and sign a conduct contract. Clear expectations and concomitant consequences for breaking any part of the contract are a must. Remind students to maintain proper field behavior and environmental courtesies:

1. Use litter containers or pack your litter out.
2. Don't taste, don't touch, don't drink, don't collect unless told to do so.
3. Touch and pick up only things related to your fieldwork. If you move animals to an observation site, return them to the place of capture when you are done.
4. If you pick up or turn over a log, rock, or board, put it back in the same place.
5. Show regard for others—don't run, push, shove, or shout or make undue noise.
6. Show regard for the habitat; don't throw rocks, break branches, stomp grasses, poke or prod. Stay out of heavy vegetation to prevent damaging it and to avoid getting cuts, scratches, or insect bites.

Before going back inside, take roll, inventory your equipment, and check the area for litter.

Preparation

If students are not comfortable, it will not be fun to be outdoors. Sometimes they will get dirty, cold, and wet. They should understand and come equipped with proper clothing and attitude. Students should have clothes that will keep them cool or warm and dry. Give students adequate notice so they come dressed and prepared on the days involved.

Different habitats require different clothing. If wandering in mowed, cleared areas, students should wear closed-toed shoes and long socks that are pulled up. Hats and shirts with sleeves will protect skin from the sun. If students will be in wooded areas or abandoned fields, they should wear long pants with socks pulled up over pant legs and insect repellent. If you have ticks in your grassy areas, check exposed areas of the skin when you return.

Encourage your PTA to purchase rubber boots and inexpensive raincoats for students. Inexpensive gloves are a must in cold weather. Have a fashion show several days before your first field studies to show all students the types of clothes you expect them to have. Have a dress rehearsal. Provide clothes for students who do not have them.

If you plan to go off school grounds on a regular basis to an empty field, pond, or park, have parents sign a generic field trip slip that allows you to take students to sites that are within a one-mile radius of your school. Communicate with parents your learning objectives and your plans to take kids outside. Find out their expertise. Invite parents to help. The more eyes and ears for supervision the better. Kids can wander farther and do more if you have support.

Hints on Learning at Your School Site

The first few occasions outside should be short. Clearly define objectives and directions. Always have a definite purpose for taking the classroom outside. Design some sort of sharing or use for the outside information. Field study journals, presentations, art projects, experiments, more research to find answers to questions generated while outside are some ideas. Have well defined roles within groups; all members should be actively employed with a task to accomplish and share. As students gain experience outside and master good behavior, then you can allow longer, more productive sessions.

Focus the student's attention without delay. Have a plan and an objective—but within the plan, be flexible. Involve everyone. Set the tone. Ask questions, point out sights and sounds. Interact and react. Teach less and share more. Don't be afraid to share your thoughts and experiences about the tall fir tree or small ant nest. Wonder how the tree got here. What has it seen during its life? How can it get enough nutrients when the ground is so hard and the parking lot so near? Who calls that tree home? How do you feel about having that tree greet you every morning, supplying your oxygen and providing shade during the summer and during the winter, turning that pounding rain into fine mist? Ask students to share previous experiences, give their opinions, and reflect individually and within groups as the outdoor session continues.

Be prepared with back-up plans. Be willing to "shoot from the hip" if the weather is bad, you could not find prime materials, or students behave in a way that dictates a change. Relax and enjoy the time outside. Students learn by example.

Be sure to visit the site beforehand. Susan can still remember various field sites on and around the middle school where she taught. One was San Mar Pond. Students spent days in life science class learning how to collect, test, measure and observe pond critters, practicing for the big trip. They inflated rubber rafts; inventoried our buckets, nets, and clip boards; divided into working teams; and set off for the pond one fine fall day. After a fifteen-minute trek to the five-acre pond, the first students announced very loudly that it was completely dry! Students are probably still talking about that trip fifteen years later!

Your school's location will determine the types of environments that will be available to study. Schools vary greatly in the size and type of available wildlife habitat. Lucky for you if you have a vacant lot, meadow, stream, or woods, but it is possible to do field studies in a completely urban environment. Urban school yards may have house sparrows, gray squirrels, and bats. Rural school yards may attract species such as the cottontail rabbit, which require extensive open space.

Even on asphalt or cement, the cracks in the sidewalk gather dust and dirt and seeds germinate and grow. An English sparrow courting in a city park or on a city street displays for his mate, and the young beg for food in a nest on top of a telephone pole. An alley cat stalks a starling. A dog forages for food. A small tree or plant bends to seek light. Under a discarded board, brick, or tire, ground creatures perform the same as their relatives under a log in the forest. A tin can filled with rain water has mosquito larvae. Students can observe food chains by observing cockroaches, predatory centipedes, scavenger sow bugs, vegetarian or scavenger ants. Weeds can attract bees or butterflies, and even water running down city streets can invite discussion of storm drains, pollution, contaminants, and water for life.

If you live in a part of the United States where there are definite seasons, the activities in this book will be most successful at certain times of the year. The fall or spring would be the best time to do the activities involving active spiders or insects. Fall is the season to find the wild fruit including berries, seeds dispersing, migrations, changing leaves, and animals preparing for winter. During the winter, some birds migrate, some mammals hibernate, and many cold-blooded animals become inactive. Some of the activities in this book can be adapted. Investigate galls (wintering home of insects); study ways some animals change color in the winter; investigate animal signs, winter buds, and squirrel and chipmunk behavior. During the early spring watch for skunk cabbage, red currant, pussy willows, coltsfoot, Indian plum, and other plants that flower before they leaf. Listen to bird songs on tape, then listen to bird songs outside. What do they mean? Make a nature calendar of the seasons in your area. Include migratory birds, year round residents, birds at feeders and baths, butterflies at flowers and mineral seeps, and so on.

Look closely at your school yard. What parts are good for studies? What types can you use? Many school yards are dirt and cement. There are very few living things. What can you do?

Search around plant roots, under leaves, logs, rocks, boards, and in the bark of trees. Look in bottles or cans for little creatures of all kinds. Look for signs such as holes, tunnel entrances, chewed limbs or stems, chewed bark, droppings, and tracks. Look at snags, tree dens and cavities, brush, and rock piles. Examine water retention ponds, ditches, landscape planting, bird baths, nest boxes, food plots or gardens, berry-producing shrubs, nut trees, feeders, or feeding stations. If you are fortunate, explore meadows, mature forests, or natural ponds. Compost piles, logged areas, ground cover, evergreens, small trees, prunings, piles of clippings or leaves also yield signs of life. Look at various layers as in the tree canopy and on and under a boulder. Explore edges of fields, forests and parking lots.

As a record of all their activities, ask students to create a neighborhood community scrapbook that includes information on the following:

1. Discussion of plants and animals that answers the following questions: What plants and animals are found in the community? Which are native and which have been introduced? Are the plants and animals affected by the human community and its activities? Give examples of how the plants and animals affect the human community. Are there any hunting, trapping, or fishing laws? Are there any pest problems such as rats, cockroaches, or coyotes?
2. A discussion of soil types and fertility
3. A discussion of how the community got there and why the site was chosen
4. A discussion of the roles people and nature played in influencing where the town was built
5. A discussion of the effects of the town on the community's natural and human resources

6. A description of the town's shape and location and a discussion of the reasons the town is shaped that way

7. A statement of the number of people who live in the community and whether it is part of a larger community or city

8. An explanation of ways the land in town is used

9. A thorough discussion of any serious land use problems such as erosion, landslides, or floods

10. The geological history of the community

11. Any special geological features and ways in which they affect the town's climate

12. Rocks and minerals found nearby, how they got there, and what roles they play in the development of the town

13. The rivers, streams, or lakes that are located in or near the community, including a tracing of the flow of water, results of chemical and biological tests, the community's sources of water, method of treatment, and sewage system

14. The condition of the air and sources of pollution

15. A statement regarding the level of noise pollution

16. The sanitation and recycling system, if any

17. The industries and ways they use natural resources

18. Community planners and development

19. The community's main source of income

20. The conservation and environmental problems

Students write poems or short stories and draw in their scrapbooks. You might use the scrapbooks in a culminating experience such as a science night and lend them to local libraries or city councils. Show them to parents, other teachers, principals, and local school board members as a way of sharing everything your students have learned in their forays into the school yard.

1
Observation

Using one or more of the five senses to gather information

The purpose of life, after all, is to live it, to taste experience to the utmost, to reach out eagerly and without fear for newer and richer experience.

—Eleanor Roosevelt

I like going outside because I can see and understand all of the chains that make up the Earth. I also think of myself as a naturalist because if I see something that interests me, like a sea urchin, I want to know what it feels like, smells like and everything about it.

—Student

School Grounds Scavenger Hunt

Process Skills Used:

observation, data collection

Purpose:

To distinguish among objects based on their physical properties, especially shape and color

National Science Standards

9C: Shapes such as circles, squares, and triangles can be used to describe many things that can be seen.

2A: Circles, squares, triangles, and other shapes can be found in nature.

Literature Entry Point

Silver, Donald. *One Small Square Backyard.*
ISBN: 0-07-05790-X

Wonderfully illustrated sections of a backyard that show above and below the grass and dirt. If used before the students go outside it will encourage them to look closely at their own backyards.

Grades
1 through 3

Duration
30 to 40 minutes

Materials
- ❑ data sheet
- ❑ clipboard
- ❑ pencil
- ❑ crayons
- ❑ hand lens (optional)

Site
School yard

Intelligences Used
naturalist
interpersonal
visual-spatial
mathematical-logical

Background

Physical properties are the observable characteristics of an object. One aspect of physical properties is the shape of the object. Examples of standard geometric shapes are squares, circles, triangles, and rectangles.

Before You Leave the Classroom

Review geometric shapes with students. Give them examples of things in nature that have those shapes. Explain that they are to look on the school grounds for additional nature items that have the shapes and colors they are studying.

Pair students. Hand out data sheets and clipboards. Ask students to color appropriate areas, if necessary. Remind them of field etiquette and your expectations when outside. Let students know that the purpose of the lesson is to focus carefully to observe and collect the data required on the sheet.

In the Field

Allow students to explore the school grounds. Give them some landmarks and ask them to stay in that area; they should make sure they can see you at all times. As students roam about, they locate objects that match descriptions on the data sheet. When they find an object, they write it down and draw a picture of it. This is a wonderful opportunity for cross-age help because younger children may find it difficult to complete the data sheet in a time you feel comfortable with. Employ older students to help collect data and record it on the data sheets. Give students some sort of signal (whistle, goose call) when you are ready for them to return to the classroom.

Back in the Classroom

Give partners time to share data with others in the class. Compile the data from the sheets and write it on one large classroom chart for further discussion and activities.

Curriculum Extensions

- Students practice writing out sentences based on what they find outside.
- Students construct books with illustrations of everything they found in one color.
- Students count all objects they found for each color, then for each shape. They make graphs to show findings.

Checking for Understanding

- Ask students to list things they saw in the outside environment and draw a picture that includes all the things on their data sheet.

Reflection Prompts

- ▶ The most interesting thing I saw today was . . .
- ▶ My favorite shape is . . .
- ▶ I think things outside are green (fill in another color) because . . .

School Grounds Scavenger Hunt Data Sheet

Name: _____

Fill out this data sheet with your partner as you make your observations on the school grounds. **Never** go somewhere that you can't see me.

Find an object that fits each description in the following boxes. Write down the name of what you see, draw a picture of it, or do both.

GREEN	SQUARE
BROWN	CIRCLE
YELLOW	TRIANGLE
BLACK	RECTANGLE

Discovering the Naturalist Intelligence, ©1999 Zephyr Press, Tucson, Arizona

Sensory Explorations

Process Skill Used:
observation, classification

Purpose:
To employ senses while observing; to become aware of the concept there are many ways in addition to using your eyes to observe

National Science Standard
6D: Learning people use their senses to find out about their surroundings and themselves. Different senses give different information.

Literature Entry Point
Boachard, David. *Voices from the Wild: An Animal Sensagoria.* ISBN: 0-81-18146-29

> *Listen, touch, smell, taste, and see the natural world as never before as twenty-five animals compete to prove that their senses are the sharpest of all.*

Background
Children need opportunities to use all their senses to gather information. The more senses students use, the more efficient they become when involved in scientific explorations. Many students have not had the opportunity to use senses other than sight to learn. Listening, smelling, and touching to understand nature opens a new world for all kids, especially those who have a strong naturalist intelligence.

Before You Leave the Classroom
To make this lesson effective, students must understand that they need to focus their concentration on the sense they are isolating from the others. Collect natural objects that have definite textures and smells, and place them in a box or paper bag. Ask students to guess what the textured objects are by only touching them, then to brainstorm and record descriptors of how the items feel. Ask students to guess what the other objects are by only smelling them, then to brainstorm and record descriptors for how the items smell. Play a nature tape and ask students to identify what they hear.

In the Field
Briefly review your expectations and required outside behavior. Since it is difficult to listen patiently and quietly in large groups, ask for parent volunteers so you can work in small groups. Select three different sites outside. Ask students to use the data sheet to list what they hear, smell, feel, and see at each site; they also list descriptors for each item.

Grades
1 through 6

Duration
30 minutes in classroom, 30 minutes outside

Materials
- ❑ box or sack of examples from nature collected from the school yard (rocks, leaves, cones, and so on)
- ❑ audiotape of wildlife sounds
- ❑ audiotape player
- ❑ clipboard
- ❑ data sheet

Site
School yard and grounds

Intelligences Used
naturalist
verbal-linguistic
bodily-kinesthetic
visual-spatial

Back in the Classroom

As a class, record on a chalkboard or butcher paper some descriptors students used on their data sheets. Discuss the difficulty of identifying sounds and smells. What words on the list provide vivid images? Highlight students' favorites. Brainstorm the conditions that are necessary for good observation (concentration, time, and few distractions). Ask them why it is difficult to listen for specific sounds outside. Ask them to write individual descriptive paragraphs about something they encountered. They will incorporate words from their own data sheets.

Curriculum Extensions

- Students use descriptors to write cinquains or other forms of poetry.
- Students write stories by becoming one of the objects they smelled, felt, heard, or saw outside.

Checking for Understanding

- Students read their compositions out loud, asking others to identify the sensory words used and draw pictures that match the students' compositions.

Reflection Prompts

- ▶ The most unique thing I heard today was . . .
- ▶ I think the sense of touch is important because . . .

Sensory Explorations Data Sheet

Name: _____

What do you *see*?

Site 1	Descriptor
Site 2	Descriptors
Site 3	Descriptors

What do you *hear*?

Site 1	Descriptors
Site 2	Descriptors
Site 3	Descriptors

What do you *smell*?

Site 1	Descriptor
Site 2	Descriptors
Site 3	Descriptors

What do you *feel*?

Site 1	Descriptors
Site 2	Descriptors
Site 3	Descriptors

Touching Ten

Process Skillsl Used:

observation, communication

Purpose:

To experience ways to observe using touch

National Science Standard

4D: Structure of Matter. Objects can be described in terms of the materials they are made of and their physical properties.

Literature Entry Point

Carter, David. *Feely Bugs.*
ISBN: 0-684-80119

This book allows the reader to feel various textures on the backs of various bugs. Lots of tactile fun.

Grades
1 through 6

Duration
50 minutes

Materials
❑ paper
❑ pencil
❑ clipboard
❑ data sheet

Site
School yard or grounds

Intelligences Used
naturalist
bodily-kinesthetic
verbal-linguistic
visual-spatial

Background

Because we rely on all of our other senses to such a large degree, the sense of touch may seem insignificant to students. But things are fuzzy and prickly for a reason. Fuzz on a dusty miller keeps the plant warm, and spines on a cactus break up air currents so the water doesn't evaporate easily during transpiration. When the smoothness of a leaf allows water to efficiently run off and not harm a plant, texture becomes very important in the natural world.

Before You Leave the Classroom

Review observation skills that use the senses. Reiterate that many people think observation means looking only. Concentrate on the sense of touch. Brainstorm a list of words to get students started; possibilities include soft, hard, rough, smooth, warm, and cold. List ten such words at the top of the data sheet. Review behavior you expect students to display outside. They touch only, not peel, break, and so on. Review and remind students of outside procedures.

In the Field

On the data sheet, students list ten things with various textures. They write down the objects and a word to describe the texture of each. For example, a student might write, "Bark is bumpy."

Back in the Classroom

Confirm and help identify items students touched. Add to the class brainstormed list the new words students used. Students individually select one item and draw a picture of it that focuses on the detail of its texture. They then write explanations of their illustrations, including the words they used on their data sheet and underlining those words.

Curriculum Extensions

- Students use their sense of smell as their focal point and individually act out objects and their scents.
- Students make up a plant or tree that would fit in their environment, draw a picture of it, and give it a name.
- Students write an explanation of why their chosen objects feel the way they do.

Checking for Understanding

- Students illustrate several objects they touched during the field study and list three words that describe texture; however, only one of the words is correct. They trade with partners and test one another.
- Place collected objects in a bag. Hand out one to each student to touch for one minute. Place the item in a bag with about eight to ten other items. Students then reach into the bag to select the item they explored.

Reflection Prompts

- ▶ The weirdest thing I touched today was . . .
- ▶ The object that had the texture I liked best was . . .
- ▶ The best part of being outside is . . .

Touch Ten Data Sheet

Name: _____

List ten words from classroom discussion in the first ten spaces.
Then write down the name of objects you find outside and a word to describe the texture of each.

1. _____   6. _____

2. _____   7. _____

3. _____   8. _____

4. _____   9. _____

5. _____   10. _____

Object   ### Texture

1. _____   _____

2. _____   _____

3. _____   _____

4. _____   _____

5. _____   _____

6. _____   _____

7. _____   _____

8. _____   _____

9. _____   _____

10. _____   _____

Discovering the Naturalist Intelligence, ©1999 Zephyr Press, Tucson, Arizona

School Yard Bingo

Process Skills Used:

observation, classification, data collection

Purpose:

To closely observe common items found in the school yard

National Science Standard

1B: People can often learn about things around them just by observing carefully.

Literature Entry Point

Harvey, Gail. *Poems of Creatures Large and Small.* ISBN: 0-517-05234-1

A book of short poems that inspires us to stop and take in the many features of the little creatures of the world along with the larger, more visible ones.

Grades
1 through 6

Duration
30 to 40 minutes

Materials
❑ pencils
❑ bingo card data sheet

Site
School yard

Intelligences Used
naturalist
mathematical-logical
verbal-linguistic
visual-spatial

Background

This activity motivates students to observe closely the many living things that are part of the school yard. This lesson can either introduce the concept of observation or assess what students have learned after you have covered the many ways observation can take place. We have enclosed the bingo cards so you have the flexibility to create observation cards based on your school grounds.

Before You Leave the Classroom

Hand out the School Yard Bingo cards and explain that the goal is to find the items listed or pictured (depending on the Bingo card you use). When students have found each item, they mark the appropriate box. You might also ask students to draw each item in the appropriate square if you are using the Bingo cards with words. Students can either complete the cards individually or in groups of two or three. Remember to review safety rules for outdoors. Also note that they need to be patient—observing takes a little time.

In the Field

Give students approximately fifteen minutes to locate various items on the bingo card. You might want to lead them to a few areas in the school yard so that they may identify most of the items on their cards.

Back in the Classroom

Take a moment to review and discuss students' experiences. Discuss the items that were easy to identify and why (for example, they were bigger, students were more familiar with them). Ask what items were more challenging to find and why (for example, they were smaller, they were under other things, they were up in the air). Explain that good observers look up and down and under things to discover all the neat things that make up the outdoors.

Curriculum Extensions

- Word Bingo: Students work individually or in small groups to make a Bingo card of names of things they have observed in the school yard.
- Picture Bingo: Pass out blank Bingo cards to the students. List items that are commonly found in the school yard and display the list. Ask students to draw pictures of the listed items in the squares in any order. Collect the cards, shuffle them, pass them out to various groups before going on your school yard hike. Students discover the items on their uniquely created cards.
- Students write poems or letters to someone in another class about the various things one can see on a hike through the school yard.
- Students use the information on the Bingo cards to create story problems using addition, subtraction, multiplication, or division.
- Students tally the number of each item they see, then share and average their data, creating a bar, line, or pie graph.

Checking for Understanding

- Create a paper and pencil test or ask students to write a poem or short paragraph that describes the qualities of a good observer.

Reflection Prompts

- ▶ The neatest things I saw in the school yard were . . .
- ▶ While playing School Yard Bingo I learned these things about being a good observer:
- ▶ If I could have changed any thing about School Yard Bingo, I would . . .

School Yard Bingo Data Sheet

Name: _____

Leaf	Bird	Seed	Fence
Rock	Bug	Dirt	Clouds
Branch	Sun	Grass	Playground toys
Flower	Moss	Worm	Bush

School Yard Picture Bingo Data Sheet

Name: _____

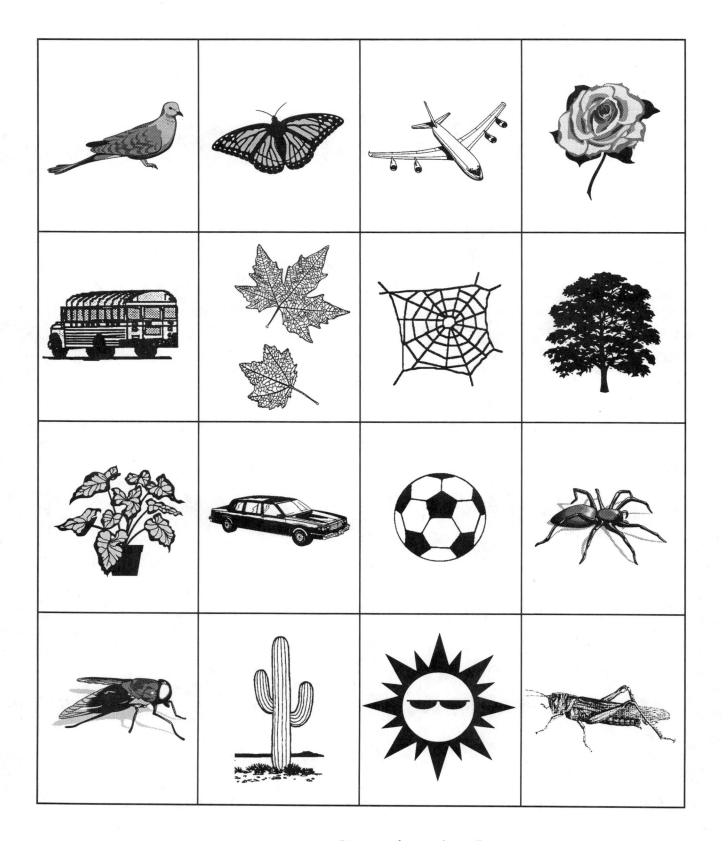

Fill in the Blank Bingo Data Sheet

Name: _____

A Quick Quadrat

Process Skills Used:

observation, data collection, prediction

Purpose:

To observe and categorize items found in a selected quadrat on the playground

National Science Standard

5A: Things can be sorted into groups in many different ways using various features to decide which things belong to which group.

Literature Entry Point

Silver, Donald. *One Small Square Woods.*
ISBN: 0-7167-6610-8

A beautifully designed and illustrated book the focus of which is on small sections of the forest floor and canopy. It shows in great detail what small things live there.

Grades
1 through 6

Duration
30 to 40 minutes

Materials
- ❑ clipboard
- ❑ string
- ❑ pencil
- ❑ measuring tape
- ❑ hand lens or loupe (optional)
- ❑ data sheet

Site
School grounds

Intelligences Used
naturalist
mathematical-logical
visual-spatial
interpersonal
intrapersonal

Background

A quadrat is a marked rectangular area. You can use yarn, string, or wood to designate your quadrats. This lesson reinforces observation skills by getting students to focus on one small area. That area is a representation of what lives in the surrounding area.

Before You Leave the Classroom

Cut yarn or string into forty-inch lengths. Ask students to use the yarn to make ten-inch squares on their desktops. Explain what a quadrat is and that it is designed for close observation. Older students can discuss area, perimeter, and square inches. Explain that students are going to construct a quadrat on the playground and record things they see inside it. As a class, list predictions of the kinds of things they will see.

In the Field

Guide students to a spot on the playground where they will likely find a variety of natural creatures and objects. Have them construct their quadrats, then count and record on their data sheets what they see. Ask them to draw on the data sheet what they observe in the quadrat.

Back in the Classroom

Pair students to share the results, then gather as a class to share. Note the things they correctly predicted they would see. Also note what was out there that they didn't have on their list. Record at least one object from everyone's square to give students an idea of what is representative of the larger area. Discuss the similar and different objects recorded.

Curriculum Extensions

- Students write sentences that explain the items they counted and illustrated in the quadrat.
- Students make pictographs of the contents of the quadrat.
- Students write story problems that require adding and subtracting contents of the quadrat.
- Students enlarge the quadrats to observe more objects.

Checking for Understanding

- Demonstrate setting up a quadrat. Duplicate it in another area of the school yard.
- Using their own quadrat data, ask students to make predictions about the kinds and numbers of things they all will find.

Reflection Prompts

▶ Today I saw . . .
▶ One thing I thought was curious was . . .
▶ I will look more closely the next time I . . .

A Quick Quadrat Data Sheet

Name: _____

Go outside. Make a square on the ground with your piece of yarn. Make sure you pick a place that has a variety of things. Draw in the corresponding sections of your data sheet the things you find in your quadrat. Identify various types of things and count them, recording them on your data sheet.

Draw

Record

Things					
Number					

Natural Collages

Process Skills Used:

> **observation,** data collection

Purpose:

> To observe and collect data on various leaf shapes and edges or other plant items abundant in your area

National Science Standard

> **5A:** Some animals and plants are alike in the way they look and in the things they do, and others are very different from one another.

Literature Entry Point

> Jeunesse, Gallinard. *Trees and Forests.*
> ISBN: 0-590-46739-4
>
> *This well-illustrated book is filled with facts about forests and the plants and animals that live in that habitat.*

Grades
1 through 6

Duration
30 minutes outside,
30 minutes inside

Materials
- ❏ various samples of deciduous leaves or other items indigenous to your area
- ❏ art paper
- ❏ colored pencils or crayons

Site
Anywhere on the school grounds where there are various types of leaves

Intelligences Used
naturalist
visual-spatial

Background

> Climate and soils determine where different types of trees grow. Deciduous trees are trees that lose their leaves. Many types of deciduous trees exist and one can identify them by their shape, bark color and texture, and leaf shape. The leaves produced by certain trees can be classified into four groups based on shape. These edges are smooth, lobed, toothed, and wavy.

Before You Leave the Classroom

> Go over background information with students. Show them examples of leaf shapes and leaf edges. Review behaviors that you expect when outside, especially never collecting anything that is healthy and alive, such as a leaf still growing on a tree. Explain clearly the purpose of the lesson and explain collection procedures. Students should handle fallen leaves carefully and select samples that are entire leaves, sturdy enough to survive the trip back to the classroom.

In the Field

> Take students on a walking tour of the playground. Encourage them to collect a wide variety of leaves. Remind students to pay attention to leaf edges.

Back in the Classroom

> Ask students to place leaves on their desktops in categories based on their edges. Students explain why leaves are shaped the way they are (collecting sunlight, preventing being eaten, keeping in warmth). You may want students to press the leaves. On heavy weight white art

paper, students make a design by tracing around leaf edges. They might choose to overlap the leaves as in the example on page 21. Using fall or natural colors, students fill in the sections of their designs with solid colors, lines, or dots. Display the designs on a bulletin board and continue to discuss them occasionally.

Curriculum Extensions

- Students write creative stories about ways leaves develop their distinctive edges and why they develop the edges.
- Students write lyrics about fall leaves to the tune of "London Bridge Is Falling Down," including the words *toothed, wavy, lobed,* and *smooth.*

Checking for Understanding

- Students present their natural collages to the class and point out the types of leaves they traced.
- After students have traced the leaves, collect them and have students categorize them by edge shape at a station set up in the classroom.
  You may even want them to use reference books to identify the leaves.

Reflection Prompts

- ▶ Today we . . .
- ▶ I now understand that . . .
- ▶ My favorite leaf shape is . . .

Natural Collages Data Sheet

Name: _____

Use leaves you find on the playground to make drawn collages. Draw around and overlap them when appropriate. Fill in shapes with solid colors, blended colors, dots, lines, or any other design that pleases your eye. Choose seasonal or other natural colors.

◄ Example of overlapped leaves

Nature's Music

Process Skills Used:

observation, analysis

Purpose:

To prepare a musical composition from sounds provided by nature and items collected from the school grounds

National Science Standard

9B: Similar patterns may show up in many places in nature and in things people make.

Literature Entry Point

Bartlett, T. C. *Tuba Lessons.*
ISBN: 015-201643-0

A young boy journeys through the woods on his way to his tuba lessons and becomes sidetracked by all the animals that want to hear him play. He encounters all kinds of helpful music along the way.

Grades
3 through 6

Duration
60 minutes

Materials
- ❏ sticks
- ❏ rocks
- ❏ leaves
- ❏ other creative noise makers students collect from nature and the playground.

Site
Classroom and school grounds

Intelligences Used
naturalist
musical-rhythmic
bodily-kinesthetic

Background

In the world around us are many sounds we don't pay attention to. Students can improve their discriminatory hearing through practice. A rustling sound could be dried leaves or a small animal, while a breaking twig could be the wind or a deer walking.

Before You Leave the Classroom

Discuss students' past experiences with the sounds of nature. What does it sound like when they walk through leaves? How many different sounds can they make when they throw rocks into ponds or lakes? What does the wind sound like when it moves through a forest?

Brainstorm a list of natural objects that make interesting sounds. Which objects could be found on the playground or school property? Ask students to select from the list objects to look for outside so they don't all come in with rocks.

In the Field

Students help one another find designated objects to use as musical instruments. Remind them to investigate the grounds to see if there is anything else to make music with that they hadn't thought of using before.

Back in the Classroom

Individually students demonstrate their nature instrument for the class. Then they work together to perform familiar tunes such as "Twinkle, Twinkle, Little Star." Next, students perform songs, such as "Row, Row, Row Your Boat," in rounds with similar-sounding instruments played for each round. Students decide which instruments should be grouped together.

Curriculum Extensions

■ Use material found inside the classroom to compose school room symphonies.

Checking for Understanding

■ Group students in teams of four with four different nature sounds. They practice and perform a familiar song. In the same groups, students create original compositions to perform.

Reflection Prompts

▶ What real instrument (flute, drum, and so on) does your nature instrument resemble or sound like?

▶ Why did you choose this object?

▶ My favorite sound was . . .

Wonders of Clouds

Process Skills Used:

observation, data collection, classification

Purpose:

To observe and identify various types of clouds while learning what clouds are made of

National Science Standard

4B: When liquid water disappears, it turns into gas (vapor) in the air and can reappear as a liquid when cooled, or as a solid if cooled below the freezing point of water. Clouds and fog are made of tiny droplets of water.

Literature Entry Point

Barrett, Judi. *Cloudy with a Chance of Meatballs.*
ISBN: 068975149-5

A delightful story of the various types of weather and how they are related to the foods we eat.

Background

Clouds are formed when water vapor in the air reaches its dew point and condenses into water droplets. There are many different clouds that are created in the sky through this process. Cirrus clouds are the delicate, feathery clouds that are generally high up in the sky. Altostratus clouds look very thin and fibrous; you can hardly tell they are there. Nimbostratus clouds are the dark gray clouds you see just before a big storm; they usually blanket the sky. Cumulus clouds are the fluffy, pillowlike clouds that have a touch of gray, which tells us a storm is about to move in. Cumulus clouds can be found high in the sky or low.

Before You Leave the Classroom

The day before your outside lesson, demonstrate the formation of clouds by placing a cup of water in a clear, two-liter bottle, then placing the bottle in the window. As the water warms, it will evaporate inside the container, The vapor will begin to condense at the top of the container. When the air in the container cools, the water forms droplets, much like those that make up clouds. The top of the bottle will appear cloudy. Discuss with your students how this process reflects the way clouds are made. Next, brainstorm with your students about the different types of clouds they recall seeing. You might want students to draw the clouds and share their pictures, which will lead in well to an explanation of the names of the clouds. Prepare students to visit the school yard by telling them they will be working individually to observe and draw clouds and remind them of proper outdoor behavior.

Grades
1 through 6

Duration
30 to 40 minutes

Materials
❑ pencil
❑ data sheet

Site
School yard on a cloudy day

Intelligences Used
naturalist
verbal-linguistic
visual-spatial

In the Field

Sometimes looking up while sitting can cause neck strain, so find a place in the school yard where students can lie down to look up at the sky, then sit up to draw. It is fun to discuss what objects the clouds look like. Ask students to draw at least five different shapes or types of clouds on their data sheets.

Back in the Classroom

Students share the various cloud types they observed. Give students a few minutes to reflect on how clouds are made and on the various types that appear in the sky.

Curriculum Extensions

- Students create mobiles of various types of clouds.
- Students write songs that describe how clouds are formed and the various types of clouds.

Checking for Understanding

- Students make drawings or diagrams of water changing from liquid to gas to form clouds.
- Students identify various cloud types by name.

Reflection Prompts

- ▶ If I were a cloud I would be a _____ cloud because . . .
- ▶ I learned . . .
- ▶ I feel clouds are important because . . .

The Wonders of Clouds Data Sheet

Name: _____

Cloud Drawing	Cloud Type	Weather Prediction (optional)

My Unique Rock

Process Skills Used:

observation, classification, comparison, prediction

Purpose:

To become familiar with various types of rocks in the school yard; to observe and identify rocks' special features

National Science Standard

4C: Chunks of rocks come in many sizes and shapes, from boulders to grains of sand and even smaller.

Literature Entry Point

Baylor, Byrd. *Everybody Needs a Rock.*
ISBN: 0-689-71051-8

A fictional young boy's perspective on choosing the perfect rock for you.

Grades
1 through 3

Duration
45 minutes

Materials
❏ rocks
❏ bucket
❏ blindfolds (optional)

Site
In the classroom or outdoors

Intelligences Used
naturalist
mathematical-logical
visual-spatial

Background

The rocks on Earth's surface can be categorized into three groups: igneous, metamorphic and sedimentary. *Igneous* rocks are formed when molten magma cools. *Metamorphic* rocks are formed when older rocks are compressed; new crystals grow in the rocks and, because the crystals are under pressure, they grow in only one direction and are thus aligned. *Sedimentary* rocks are composed when weathered or eroded fragments of older rocks or remains of living organisms are compressed into several layers. You can identify rock types by their textures. Most igneous rocks have crystals. The texture of sedimentary rocks is determined by the rocks they are made of. Sandstone can be very fine grained, while conglomerates can have huge jagged or smooth pieces in them. Rocks in the school yard can be jagged (broken as in crushed gravel) or rounded by water such as a river or glacier. Rocks can travel from place to place by trucks, trains, gravel barges, dredges, and humans. Rocks can be moved in nature by volcanoes, earthquakes, landslides, rivers, glaciers, and so on. The rocks in your school yard could be local or from long distances. Check with your local United States Geological Survey office, Department of Natural Resources Geology division, or college or university for the real story on the rocks in your area. If the rocks are solid (as in cliffs, road cuts) and attached underground, they are bedrock and naturally occur in your area.

Before You Leave the Classroom

After you have reviewed the background information, tell students they will be observing and collecting rocks outside. Remind them of outdoor safety rules. Tell them they are to collect two different types of rocks that are small enough to fit inside one hand. Let them know that, when they have each collected two different rocks, they are to place the rocks in the bucket.

In the Field

Students collect rocks as described above and place them in the bucket. When every student has collected rocks and you have several kinds, return to the classroom or conduct the rest of the lesson outside. Have students individually place their hands in the bucket and draw out a rock. It does not have to be one they found. Give students time to get to know the rock they select. Tell them to look at their rock very closely. They should smell their rock, touch it with their fingers, and maybe even rub it lightly against their cheeks. When they feel they would be able to identify their rock by touch from a pile of all the others, have them place it back in the bucket. Now without looking (you may want to use blindfolds), students pass the bucket of rocks to the right, with each student feeling inside the bucket to choose his or her rock. When they have their rocks, they hold on to them but continue passing the other rocks. Once most of the students are satisfied that they have their original rocks, they open their eyes.

Back in the Classroom

Have students reflect, then discuss the following questions as a class. How many were able to identify their rock? What made identification easy or difficult? What would they do differently if they could try again? If time permits, allow students to choose another rock and go through the process a second time.

Curriculum Extensions

- Students make papier mâché models of their rocks.
- Students sort rocks into groups, count the rocks in each group, and discuss as a class why they think that type of rock was in the school yard.
- Students write a song, using the various sounds rocks can make when you hit them against one another or rub them together.

Checking for Understanding

- Working in groups, give the students ten different rocks. Have them observe each rock, then sort them based on appearance. They place the rocks in a bucket and pick out their ten rocks from the other rocks in the bucket.

Reflection Prompts

- ▶ Words I would choose to describe my rock would be . . .
- ▶ I have learned these things about rocks today . . .

Mapping the School Grounds

Process Skills Used:

observation, data collection

Purpose:

To learn how to draw a map of a school to scale

National Science Standard

9C: Shapes: The scale chosen for a graph or drawing makes a big difference how useful it is.

Literature Entry Point

George, Jean Craighead. *Who Killed Cock Robin?*
ISBN: 00-602-1981-5

An eighth grader uses an ecological map to follow a trail to figure out the environmental imbalances that have caused the death of the town's best known robin.

Background

This map will show the relationship between the built environment (school buildings, playgrounds, and parking lot) and the natural environment's significant features, such as meadows, woods, edges, and trees. Once you have the map, all the other information collected about the plants and animals can be layered onto the map by drawing it on clear plastic overlays, much like global information systems are organized on a computer.

Before You Leave the Classroom

You can easily tie mapping in with math, geography, and community and state history. Old National Geographic maps are ideal for preliminary study because they include maps of galaxies, the ocean floor, historical events, national parks, and other areas of interest. Usually, every child will find a map that interests her. Encourage students to bring in specialized maps of places they have been or want to go. Even a map of Disney World would have the basic features you'll want to cover. Introduce features such as legend, scale, and color. We always start by asking students to measure objects in the classroom, arms, shoe prints, books, 3-ring binders, desks, doorways, and so on. You are welcome to use the metric system. Students transfer these straight line measurements to a piece of graph paper; each square represents one inch. After they understand the concept of scale, they map their bedrooms. They find the longest distance in the room first, count the number of squares on the graph paper, and figure out what each square will most appropriately represent. Make sure students use the entire piece of graph paper instead of having a tiny little drawing up in one corner. This exercise is an effective way to see if students really understand scale; when they

Grades
4 through 6

Duration
200 minutes

Materials
- ❏ graph paper (the largest grid you can find)
- ❏ tape measure or meter and yard sticks (inexpensive flexible cloth tape measures work great)
- ❏ clipboards
- ❏ pencils
- ❏ compass
- ❏ ruler or other straight edge

Site
School yard or nearby park

Intelligences Used
naturalist
bodily-kinesthetic
visual-spatial

show that the length of their bedroom is sixteen feet and that their bed is ten feet long or their doorway is only one foot wide, you know they don't quite understand. The next step is to use graph paper to map their houses. Our students love the follow-up assignment of mapping their dream homes. Once these assignments are completed with lots of TLC and feedback from you, students go on to the real project—mapping the school grounds. If you would like to take a short cut, obtain a blueprint of the school grounds from the district engineering department, maintenance department, or grounds crew, then add the natural features you find important: soil types, vegetation (canopy, ground cover, middle layers, landscaping plants, indigenous plants, wetland plants, and so on), animals and animal sign, seasonal changes, and yearly changes.

In the Field

Because it would be very awkward to use a tape measure to measure the long distances in a school yard, students must measure their pace. Set up two points one hundred feet apart on the playground for students to walk purposefully and normally between, counting the number of steps they take. They repeat the process until they come out with the same number of steps for three trials in a row. They divide this number (usually about 35 to 45) into 100, which is the length of their paces. Now they can measure as they walk. If a pace is 2.6 feet, then students count the number of paces it takes to walk around a certain element, multiply the number by 2.6, and draw the element to scale on the graph paper. Be sure students align their maps with north at the top. Work as a class to figure out which way north is. Find the longest element in the school yard, figure out the scale, and draw the longest perimeter line on the graph paper. Make sure the scale will allow students to draw everything on their map and to fill the paper. Draw all perimeter lines, then draw the main building. If there are objects (shrubs, trees, other classes in progress) that prevent students from pacing off right next to the building, demonstrate how to pace out a prescribed distance from the building, then walk in a straight line to intersect. If you have long halls and it's unfavorable weather outside, you can pace from one end of the school to the other on the inside.

Back in the Classroom

Students finalize their maps. If a blueprint is available, they can compare it with their own work. Ask students to come up with ways they can verify the accuracy of their maps. For instance, if the hallway is larger than the classroom, something is wrong. If you take individual student maps, make overheads, and layer them—are they all the same? Why not? Discuss common errors.

Checking for Understanding

- Students write the steps they took to create their maps. They include recommendations for further study and for changes in the procedure.
- Two student teams pair up, compare maps, and iron out any inconsistencies, which may require remeasuring.

Curriculum Extensions

- As a natural extension to this school map, create maps of the community. Find your ecological address (for example, South Bay Elementary School, Woodland Creek Estuary, Henderson Inlet Watershed, Puget Sound Basin, West Coast, United States). Just as a

postal address helps the post office deliver things to your home, you can develop your own community address. Your watershed's streams, rivers, and lakes including those that empty into the ocean, estuary or bay with all of the land (farms, towns, mountains) around these waterways should be included.

- Read, compare, and contrast maps of all kinds—topography maps, road maps, city utility maps, zoning maps, population maps, soil maps, and habitat maps all give information about your community.

Reflection Prompts

▶ I felt frustrated when . . .

▶ I thought the best part was _____ because . . .

▶ I liked working in a group because . . .

▶ I would like to change the way my group worked by . . .

▶ The next project I would like to map is . . .

2

Data Collection

Gathering information through observations
and measurements in a systematic way.

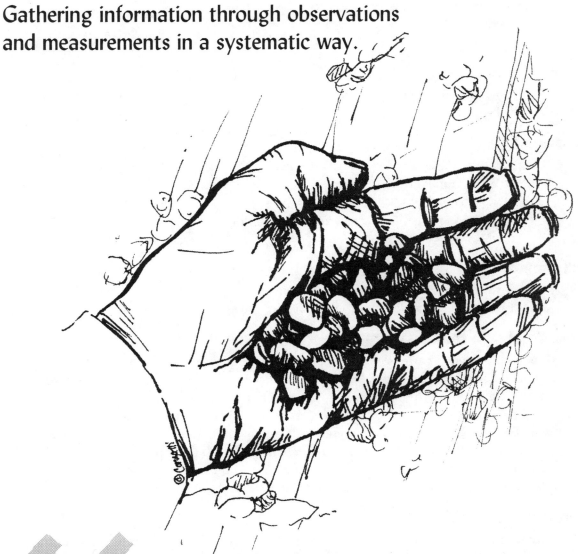

There is not a sprig of grass that shoots uninteresting to me, nor anything that moves.

—Aldo Leopold

I think the outside is a great place to learn because it doesn't have the four walls like the classroom we are in day after day.

—Student

Alphabet Hike

Process Skills Used:

data collection, observation

Purpose:

To collect data based on visual observations made in the outside environment and integrate the data into language arts

National Science Standard

1B: People can often learn about things around them by observing carefully.

Literature Entry Point

Jecan, Gauriel, Karen Pandell, Nancy Sheehan, and Art Wolff. *Animal Action ABC*.
ISBN: 0525-45486-1

Photographs of animals in action labeled with alliteration (leopards leaping).

Grades
1 through 3

Duration
30 minutes

Materials
❏ data sheet
❏ paper
❏ pencils
❏ dictionary
❏ hand lens (optional)

Site
Playground and vicinity

Intelligences Used
naturalist
verbal-linguistic
mathematical-logical
visual-spatial

Background

When conducting visual observations, it is easy to focus on large, easily seen elements. Students need guided practice to recognize details and specific characteristics.

Before You Leave the Classroom

Model for students various examples of ways to use their eyes to observe. Don't just scan at eye level. Bend down and look for things under rocks ands leaves. Look upward into the sky and treetops to find the wonderful things they have to share.

Remind students to use all their senses during the observations. They will work in pairs, possibly with an older student, to collect data. Explain that they may not see or hear something for each letter, but they will accumulate items for as many letters as possible. They may list more than one item per letter depending on your purpose. You may want them to graph the occurrences of various letters, for example.

In the Field

Guide students to locations where they will find items in nature to match the letters. Allow them fifteen minutes to draw to collect their data.

Back in the Classroom

Discuss the letters and objects recorded. Ask students to check spelling; introduce the dictionary, if necessary. Students may practice handwriting by recopying the data list or appropriate words you pull for the data sheet. Target specific letters, possibly letters for which students found the most and least items. Graph the occurrences of various letters.

Curriculum Extensions

- Students look for numbers in nature. They might find a branch with five leaves or an ant with six legs. They find an object for each number 1 through 10.
- Students go on a color hike.
- Students make alphabet books that illustrate some of the collected items
- Students write stories about outside adventures that include items they listed on their data sheets. They underline the items in their stories.

Checking for Understanding

- Students match, recall, or draw as many things from the list as possible.
- Students write sentences using words from the hike list.

Reflection Prompts

▶ I saw . . .

▶ I want to learn more about . . .

▶ My favorite thing on the list was

_____

because . . .

Alphabet Hike Data Sheet

Name: _____

As you hike outside, list all the things you see and hear on the lines by the letters the items begin with (*leaf* will go by *l*, for example). Try to find at least one item for every letter in the alphabet. (Good luck with *x* and *z!*)

Remember—
- Respect the environment around you in the ways we have discussed.
- Be very quiet so everyone can hear sounds.

A _____   N _____

B _____   O _____

C _____   P _____

D _____   Q _____

E _____   R _____

F _____   S _____

G _____   T _____

H _____   U _____

I _____   V _____

J _____   W _____

K _____   X _____

L _____   Y _____

M _____   Z _____

Total objects found: _____

Acting Out the Water Cycle

Process Skills Used:

data collection, communication

Purpose:

To "become" various parts of the water cycle and understand their relationships to one another

National Science Standard

4B: When water disappears, it turns into a gas (vapor) in the air and can reappear as a liquid when cooled, or as a solid if cooled to the freezing point of water. Clouds and fog are made of tiny droplets of water.

Literature Entry Point

Locker, Thomas. *Water Dance.*
ISBN: 0-15-201284-2

Poetic text and beautiful pictures take you through water's constant dance. The water cycle illustrations are followed by scientific facts that relate to each drawing.

Grades
1 through 6

Duration
30 minutes

Materials
❑ cards labeled *evaporation, precipitation, condensation, transpiration, ground water*

Site
Inside or outside the classroom

Intelligences Used
naturalist
bodily-kinesthetic
interpersonal

Background

Water falls to the earth in the form of precipitation (snow, hail, sleet, or rain). Some water runs into lakes that feed streams or rivers that eventually empty into the ocean. Other water falls into lakes or ponds that don't drain or soaks into the ground. Plants and animals use some water. When water evaporates, it returns to the air in the form of a gas. When a plant gives off moisture through its leaves (like when a person sweats) it is called *transpiration*. Heat from the sun speeds up the evaporation of water. As the water vapor in the air cools, it changes from a gas into a liquid and falls to the ground.

In the Classroom

Divide the class into five groups. Secretly tell each group or hand out a card that tells them the role they will play in the water cycle. Each group devises actions and sounds that fit their role. The entire group performs their stage of the cycle for others to guess. Following are some suggestions for stages:

- Surface water sources of evaporation (lakes, rivers, ocean, and so on)
- Evaporation (from all sources, including leaves, people)
- Clouds formed by condensation
- Precipitation (all forms)
- Ground water (wells, soils) plus water taken in by trees and plant roots.

Form new groups with one representative from each original group in each new group. Students arrange themselves in the correct sequence of the water cycle. Student take turns making appropriate actions and sounds, proceeding faster and faster around the circle.

Curriculum Extensions

- Students compose a song that explains the various stages of the water cycle.
- Students perform a transpiration experiment by wrapping a plastic bag around the leafy part of a plant or the entire plant. They watch for a few days to see water condense on the bag as the plant transpires.
- Students fill a glass to a certain level and mark that level; they leave the glass in the classroom and note the rate of evaporation.

Checking for Understanding

- Administer a paper and pencil test.
- Students draw pictures of the water cycle and label the parts.
- Students write about a trip through the water cycle to use as a guided imagery.

Reflection Prompts

- ▶ In what way were you like the real water cycle?
- ▶ At what stage do you think the water cycle starts?
- ▶ I learn best when I . . .

Dirt Works

Process Skills Used:

data collection, classification

Purpose:

To learn about the characteristics of dirt, where it comes from, and how it works for the environment

National Science Standard

4C: Processes That Shape the Earth—Rock is composed of different combinations of minerals. Smaller rocks come from the breakage and weathering of bedrock and larger rocks. Soil is made partly from weathered rock, partly from plant remains, and also contains many living organisms.

Literature Entry Point

Cole, Joanna. *The Magic School Bus.*
ISBN: 0-590-40760-0

Ms. Frizzle takes her class on a field trip to the center of Earth and back again. Much geological and soil information is interspersed throughout.

Background

Soil is the loose material on Earth's surface in which plants grow. Soil is made up of crumbling rocks, decaying organisms, air, and water. Soil is an important factor in ecosystems because it supports the growth of plants and decomposers. With plenty of nutrients and plenty of moisture, soil supports many communities.

Topsoil is dark in color because it contains humus, which is formed when decomposers break down organic material (the remains of plants and animals). Humus is high in nutrients such as phosphorous and nitrogen. It takes nature 250 to 2,000 years to make one inch of topsoil. Soil that has a lot of sand allows rain to drain through, which carries away the valuable soil nutrients.

Soil that is made up of fine particles of clay is hard. The clay particles block the absorption of water.

Various soils are good for various, specific kinds of plants. Cattails, for instance, like soil that is saturated with fresh water; cranberries thrive in soil that is very acidic; and dune plants grow in sandy soil.

Characteristics of soils include color, moisture content, particle size, and texture (gritty, silky or powdery). Other adjectives to describe soil are *cohesive, sandy,* and *sticky.* Types of soil include loam, silt, clay, sand.

Grades
4 through 6

Duration
90 minutes

Materials
- ❏ paper
- ❏ pencil
- ❏ hand lenses
- ❏ screens made from netting from the store
- ❏ crayons
- ❏ large spoons or hand trowels
- ❏ plastic bags, or cups to hold soil

Site
Places around the school yard where dirt can be collected such as paths, flower beds, athletic fields, edges, meadows

Intelligences Used
naturalist
bodily-kinesthetic
mathematical-logical

Before You Leave the Classroom

Use your science book or library resource book to cover background information on weathering of rocks into soil. Review the importance of top soil in plant growth. If possible, check with your local Soil Conservation Bureau for information about soil in your area. You might also invite a speaker. The Cooperative Extension Service or Master Gardener program would be a good resource.

In the Field

Students collect soil samples from four different sites, carefully labeling each sample with the site from which they collected it. Instruct them to collect the soil from six inches below the surface.

Back in the Classroom

Students examine the samples and fill out their data sheets, noting smell, color, texture, particle size, and organic content (dead plant and animal remains). They place one-half teaspoon of each soil isolated on a white sheet of paper. From a box of crayons, students choose the color that most closely matches each soil sample and scribble that color next to the sample, writing down the name of the color from the crayon. Log the various soil colors in the correct places on the classroom map of the school grounds.

Curriculum Extensions

- Using 9-inch sections of 3-inch PVC pipe, students test how quickly a measured amount of water will soak into the ground at various sampling sites, including compacted ground, sand, flower bed, lawn.
- Students fashion a coffee filter into an inverted cone and cover a quart jar with black paper. They set the coffee filter on top of the jar, put dirt in the filter, and shine a light on the dirt. Organisms will crawl out of the dirt and escape down the cone into the jar, where they will be trapped for students to examine.
- Ask students to check with your local conservation district to find out how local soils were formed (glaciation, lake deposits, volcanoes, river depositions, and so on).
- Students use sieves, toothpicks, and small paint brushes to sort soils according to color and texture on a sheet of newspaper. They draw a simple design onto a piece of heavy paper, then use glue to trace the lines. They sprinkle the soil on the glue, using funnels or shakers to place the soil. They let the outline dry, then fill in the spaces with various types of soils, using the same procedure.

Checking for Understanding:

- Students write a syntu about soil. A syntu has five lines. Line 1 contains only one word, the name of the natural feature. Line 2 is an sensory observation about the item named in line 1; students may use only one sense. Line 3 is a thought, feeling, or evaluation about the item in line 1. Line 4 is another sensory observation about the item, using a different sense than that used in line 2. Line 5 states a one-word meaning for the item in line 1.
- Students write a recipe for 1 cup of fertile soil. What does dirt provide the environment?
- Students write an essay that answers the following questions: Why do we need soil? Of what is soil made? By what characteristics is soil classified? Give them the following facts to include in their essays: Rocks are made of minerals that nourish plants and some soil-

dwelling organisms. Worms, sow bugs, and other creatures digest plant material and the resulting wastes add material to the soil, while the movement of these critters through the soil aerates it. Aerated soil allows plants' roots and soil-dwellers to take needed oxygen from the soil. Plants' roots aerate the soil and take up nutrients, which are returned to the soil when the plant dies and decays.

Reflection Prompts

▶ I liked studying soil because . . .

▶ I didn't know this fact about soil:

▶ When I put my hands in soil I think of . . .

▶ If I were a plant, I would want this kind of soil:

Dirt Works School Yard Map

Name: _____

Draw a map in the space below and indicate the exact location of your four collection sites. Number them 1 through 4. Measure from a landmark to mark the precise locations.

Dirt Works Data Sheet

Name: _____

Soil sample	Smell	Color	Texture (rub between thumb and fingers when wet)	Particle size	Organic matter (low to high)
1					
2					
3					
4					

Our School Yard Community

Grades
1 through 6

Duration
45 minutes

Materials
❏ hand lens
❏ binoculars
❏ data sheet
❏ pencil

Site
Anywhere outside

Intelligences Used
naturalist
interpersonal
mathematical-logical
verbal-linguistic

Process Skills Used:

data collection, observation, classification

Purpose:

To observe and identify plants and animals in the school yard, classifying them into the groups producers and consumers

National Science Standards

5A: A great variety of kinds of living things can be sorted into groups in many ways using various features to decide which things belong to which group.

5D: Animals eat plants or other animals for food.

Literature Entry Point

Rosen, Michael. *All Eyes on the Pond.*
ISBN: 0-590-48412-5

This book points out the importance of observing all things, big and small, that live in a community.

Background

All the plants and animals that live in and around a school yard are part of your school yard community. A community is the living part of an ecosystem. Organisms within the school yard depend on one another. Plants exist in all communities. Plants are also called *producers.* They use the energy produced by the sun to make their food. Other parts of the community are animals that hunt other plants or animals for food. They are called *consumers.*

In the school yard, you will see producers and consumers. In most communities, nature is balanced, with just the right number of producers and consumers to ensure they all have adequate food.

Before You Leave the Classroom

Review with students the concepts of community, producers and consumers. Show students the School Yard Community List. Encourage them to draw pictures of the things they find in the school yard. Remind them of the safety rules and to respect all things outdoors.

In the Field

Students go to a variety of places in the school yard to observe. Encourage them to look up in the sky and trees as well as down on the ground, in the cracks of concrete, and in the bark of trees.

Back in the Classroom

Students draw pictures that include all the items they found and label each one as producer or consumer. Students write one short statement at the bottom of their drawing that describes a community, a producer, and a consumer.

Curriculum Extensions

■ Students write a poem or song that describes a community and the plant producers and animal consumers that live in it.

■ Students add up all the plant producers and animal consumers they discovered, then create a bar graph or pie graph using the information.

Checking for Understanding

■ Review the data sheet in class. Ask students to take the data and classify the items they observed as producers or consumers.

■ Ask students to give examples of producers and consumers other than those they found.

Reflection Prompts

▶ Today, I learned that a community is . . .

▶ My favorite part of the community is . . .

School Yard Community Data Sheet

Name: _____

Find in the school yard as many plants and animals listed below as you can. Draw an example of the neat things you discover. Be sure not to pick or collect anything. Have fun!

Description	Drawings	Producers or Consumers
At least two different kinds of leaves		
At least two different kinds of flowers		
At least two different kinds of bark		
At least two different kinds of trees		
At least two different kinds of bugs		
At least two different kinds of weeds		
At least two different kinds of birds		
At least two different signs of animals (prints, droppings, hair)		

► How many consumers did you find in your school yard?
► How many producers or plants did you find?
► Were there more consumers or producers?

Discovering the Naturalist Intelligence, ©1999 Zephyr Press, Tucson, Arizona

Plants Can't Walk

Process Skills Used:

data collection, classification, measurement

Purpose:

To observe winter weeds, collect seeds, plot weed patches, and graph information

National Standard

9B: Tables, graphs, and symbols are alternative ways of representing data and relationships that can be translated from one to another.

Literature Entry Point

Wolff, Ferida. *A Weed Is a Seed.*
ISBN: 0-395-72291-8

This story follows a family through a year of natural happenings. It explores how the same event or activity can be viewed in two different ways.

Grades
5 through 6

Duration
2 hours

Materials
❑ hand lenses
❑ graph paper
❑ string
❑ rulers

Site
A weedy area, such as flower bed, field, edge of parking lot

Intelligences Used
naturalist
visual-spatial
logical-mathematical

Background

There is no difference between a weed and a regular plant. Sometimes people call certain kinds of plants weeds because the plant is unwanted, intrusive, or non-native. Weeds can be aggressive colonizers and can quickly settle on land that has been disturbed by humans. The weeds in flower beds or vegetable gardens may be native plants that normally grow in the area the humans are trying to change. Weeds are important because they provide seeds for birds, homes for insects, and building materials for small mammals.

Before You Leave the Classroom

Place students in small groups. Review outside procedures and behaviors. Find a part of the school yard that has lots of weeds. Sometimes you can just use a landscaped area that has not been maintained. Assign each group to a plot or small section of that area. You may want to use your school map to indicate exact locations.

In the Field

Students find various weeds listed on the data sheet. If naming isn't important to you, you could have students make up their own weed names. If these weeds aren't prevalent in your area, create your own data chart with the names of weeds that grow in your area. Students look for the biggest patch of one kind of weed. They count and record the numbers of each plant. They collect seeds, pods, berries, and so forth for comparison in the classroom. They place a string around the outside of the patch and cut the string to the measurement.

Back in the Classroom

Students find the area of their weed patch by taking the length of string, folding it into four equal sections, measuring one section, and multiplying that number by itself (a patch eight feet by eight feet would be sixty-four square feet). Students share all data for all plots. They transfer information from their data sheets onto graphs. They can graph the sizes of seeds, the height of plants, the area of the plots, the number of dominant plants on different graphs. Discuss with students what might happen to animals if weeds were eliminated from your school yard.

Curriculum Extensions

- Students go on walkabout to investigate all parts of their school yard. They come up with twenty-five words that best describe the area, then group words into categories, such as words about parts of the area, words about isolated sections, words about much of the area, words about the entire area, words about their favorite areas, words that describe the best parts of the area, words that describe the worst parts of the area, and words that describe changes they would like to see in the area.
- Students imagine they are individual people who just came to this area from a place far away. They know nothing about the area other than what they can piece together from what they saw on their walkabouts. Using such evidence, they write a short story that explains what could have happened on this site over time. They may not use information they've heard from other people or read in a book or the newspaper. The stories can begin as far back as students wish but must end with the present. As much as possible, students write in sequence. They are welcome to include an illustrated time line. The characters can include living and nonliving things.

Checking for Understanding

- Make overheads of the group graphs and have groups present their findings. They work together to make any corrections. Then students exchange data sheets with another group. The new group checks the math and accuracy of the data sheet. They must show their computations. Students make graphs using this corrected data.

Reflection Prompts

- ▶ I now understand . . .
- ▶ The hardest part for me was . . .
- ▶ The part that was easy for me to do was . . .
- ▶ I had the most fun doing this part of the activity:
- ▶ I think weeds are . . .
- ▶ I learned . . .

Plants Can't Walk Data Sheet 1

Name: _____

Plant Name	Description: plant, seed, seed case, pod, fruit, berry, and so on
Dandelion	
Thistle	
Scotch broom	
Yarrow	
Queen Anne's lace	
Snow berry	
Salal	
Oregon grape	
Teasel	
Mullin	
Foxglove	

Plants Can't Walk Data Sheet 2

Name: _____

Plot number	Location	Main kind of weed	Average height of 10 plants	Number of dominant weeds	Number of other weeds	Area of weed patch

Plants Can't Walk Data Sheet 3

Name: _____

Seed drawing	Size	Color	Texture	Smell	Way it travels

Discovering the Naturalist Intelligence, ©1999 Zephyr Press, Tucson, Arizona

Spinning Spiders and Wonder Webs

Process Skills Used:
data collection, observation

Purpose:
To learn how to observe a spider at its web and look for patterns, similarities and differences between individuals of one species and their webs

National Science Standard
5A: Individuals of the same kind differ in their characteristics, behaviors, and some differences give some individuals advantages in survival and reproduction.

Literature Entry Point
Cole, Joanna. *The Magic School Bus Spins a Web: A Book about Spiders.*
ISBN: 0-590-92234-3

Ms. Frizzle and her class are at a drive-in movie. An army is trying to kill a giant praying mantis, which makes Phoebe angry. She thinks the army should just trap the big bug, not kill it. Ms. Frizzle starts up the Magic School Bus and drives right into the movie. The class learns some tricks from a master trapper—the spider.

White, E. B. *Charlotte's Web.*
ISBN: 0-06-440055-7

This popular children's classic is a great story with some good information about spiders.

Grades
1 through 6

Duration
50 minutes

Materials
❑ paper
❑ pencil
❑ small articles such as feathers, popcorn kernels, rice grains, seeds, pieces of paper, plastic beads, twigs

Site
Vacant lot, meadow or field, area with landscape shrubs, woods

Intelligences Used
naturalist
bodily-kinesthetic
visual-spatial

Background
Orb spider webs, the classic wheel with spokes that we usually think of, are just one kind of spider web. The length of silk that goes into these amazing constructions is longer than sixty feet. Many spiders have very poor eyesight but amazing abilities to feel and interpret vibrations in their webs. With every leg on the net to sense the vibrations, they can tell the location and size of victims snared in their web. When the prey is small, the spider dashes in, bites the animal, wraps it in silk threads, and eats it or saves it for another day. In order to eat the prey, the spider injects digestive juices to liquefy up the insides, then sucks them out. Large victims that pose a threat, such as a yellow jacket, will be cut loose.

Silk is produced by as many as seven glands deep inside a spider's body. It can be dry, sticky, smooth, fuzzy, thick, or thin. The silk is still liquid when it leaves the spider's body. It is very sturdy. Some types are three times stronger than the same diameter steel thread. The silk comes out of spinnerets, which are flexible, finger-like tubes near the end of the spiders body. The spinnerets pull and bend the silk.

Believe it or not, Miss Muffet was a real girl named Patience who lived during the 1500s. Her father was a spider expert and believed, as many people did, that spiders cured illness. So when Patience was sick—yes—mashed spiders!!! People were still swallowing spiders like pills for illness up to the 1800s.

Before You Leave the Classroom

Caution students about any local poisonous spiders. Remind them not to handle spiders. Divide the class into small groups. Each group should have small articles with which to test webs, such as human hair, match sticks, o-shaped cereal, fishing lure flies, plastic flies, and dead flies. Each group should have a long, slender stick with which to simulate a vibrating insect. Go over the instructions and the data sheets.

In the Field

Students locate a fresh spider web with a spider in it. They observe the web and fill out the data sheets. They gently use their sticks to simulate prey flying into the web and observe the spider's behavior.

Back in the Classroom

Students share their observations and data. As a class, discuss reasons temperature might change the way a spider behaves. How might difficulty spinning a web affect a spider's ability to survive?

Curriculum Extensions

- Students make webs out of fine thread and small nails or pins in cardboard.
- Students dust the webs with fine powder such as corn starch. They hold a sheet of black paper against the side that has been dusted and flick the web to capture its outline.
- As a trust activity, students design a 5-foot-by-6-foot web, break into teams, and work together to go through the web without touching the "silk."

Checking for Understanding

- Students write a variety of questions about spiders, including multiple choice, short answer, true and false, and fill in. Make these student-generated questions into a paper and pencil test.

Reflection Prompts

▶ I liked _____
 most about studying spiders because . . .
▶ I am most like a spider in these ways:
▶ I am least like a spider in these ways:
▶ If I found a spider in my bedroom, I would . . .

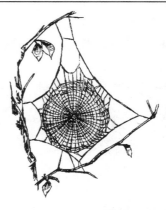

Spinning Spiders Data Sheet 1

Name: _____

What is the temperature? _____

What is the spider web attached to?

Which direction does the spider web face?

How close is the nearest web?

How large is the web?

Is the spider in or at the web?

Are there any remains of insects at the web or near the web?

Are there any insects encased in silk waiting to be dined upon?

Spinning Spiders Data Sheet 2

Name: _____

Don't destroy or break the web. If the spider is on location, gently drop various objects onto the web. Blow gently on the web.

How does the spider behave when you drop something on its web? When you blow on it?

Wiggle the web with a long, slender stick or feather; imitate a house fly.

Object	Prediction of Spider's Reaction	Actual Reaction

Discovering the Naturalist Intelligence, ©1999 Zephyr Press, Tucson, Arizona

Tall Trees

Process Skills Used:

data collection, communication

Purpose:

To gain experience with estimating and measuring height of tall objects

National Science Standard

2A: Mathematical ideas can be represented concretely, graphically, and symbolically.

Literature Entry Point

Seuss. *The Lorax.*
ISBN: 0-394-82337-0

Fanciful tale about trees and their importance to the environment.

Background

Trees provide oxygen and shade for rivers and streams. Their root systems control floods. They are homes for animals and insects. Trees produce food and offer various forms of protection for all living things.

Before You Leave the Classroom

Trees' heights can be estimated and measured in various ways. This lesson explores one way to determine the approximate height of a tree through simple measurements. Give students time to practice measuring with and reading a yardstick. Pair students. The pairs measure one partner's height in inches and record it on the data sheet (value t). Instruct them about appropriate outdoor behavior. They will select a tree in an area you have established. Equip the pairs with a yardstick, data sheet on a clipboard, and a pencil.

In the Field

Partners choose a tree, estimate its height, and write their predictions on the data sheet. The partner whose height was measured stands next to the tree. The other partner moves far enough away from the tree that the yardstick when held at arm's length appears taller than the tree. This partner measures how many inches tall the partner by the trees appears to be on the yardstick and notes it on the data sheet (value x). The partner then measures how many inches tall the tree appears to be and notes that figure on the data sheet (value y).

Back in the Classroom

Using the measurement you collected in the field, calculate the height of the tree using the instructions on the data sheet.

Grades
4 through 6

Duration
40 minutes

Materials
❏ data sheet
❏ yardstick
❏ paper
❏ pencil
❏ clipboard

Site
Any area that has trees with some surrounding space

Intelligences Used
naturalist
mathematical-logical
interpersonal
visual-spatial

Curriculum Extensions

■ Find out from a local lumber store how much a foot of board costs. Figure out how much your tree would be worth if it were cut down.

■ Research the value of the tree if it were left standing on your school grounds. How is it important to the environment?

Checking for Understanding

■ Students use graph paper to design a scale drawing of the tree and the partner.

■ Students write the instructions for determining the height of a tree. They may not refer to the data sheet.

Reflection Prompts

▶ I recommend that . . .

▶ I hope that . . .

▶ The easiest part of this activity was . . .

▶ Trees are . . .

Tall Trees Data Sheet

Name: _____

Record the height in inches of the partner you
measured. $t =$ _____

What kind of tree are you measuring?   _____

Estimate the height of the tree in feet.   _____

The partner whose height you measured stands
next to the tree. The other partner stands far
enough away so that, when the yardstick is held
at arm's length, it appears taller than the tree.
How many inches does your partner appear to be? $x =$ _____

From the same spot, record how many inches
tall your tree appears to be. $y =$ _____

Divide y by x. Record results as z. $z =$ _____

Multiply z by t (partner's height).   _____

Divide tree's height in inches by 12 to get tree's
height in feet.   _____

Comments about this activity and observations of other living outdoor things

Thunderstorm

Process Skills Used:

data collection, communication

Purpose:

To associate rhythms and patterns with various stages of a thunderstorm

National Science Standard

4B: Events in nature have a repeating pattern.

Literature Entry Point

Martin, Bill, and Joan Archanbach. *Listen to the Rain.* ISBN: 0-80-500682-6

> *Wonderful picture book provides sounds to accompany different parts of the water cycle and the precipitation that results from a thunderstorm.*

Grades
1 through 6

Duration
15 minutes

Materials
❏ none

Site
Classroom

Intelligences Used
naturalist
musical-rhythmic
bodily-kinesthetic
interpersonal

Background

The most common storms are thunderstorms. As the air rises, it cools and latent heat is released as condensation occurs. The release of heat provides energy that intensifies the upward movement of the air and develops the storm. The condensation causes cumulonimbus clouds to rise sometimes more than 15,000 feet from their base to their top. These clouds bring rain, hail, and sometimes thunder and lightning. Lightning is caused by the sudden release of accumulated static electricity in the clouds. The flash, with a current of some 10,000 amps, travels over 186,000 miles per second. The enormous amount of energy in the flash heats the air along its path to more than 60,000 degrees Fahrenheit. The violent expansion of the air molecules along the path of the lightening generates an intense sound wave—thunder. Lightning is seen before thunder is heard because light travels much faster than sound.

Discuss with students thunderstorms they have experienced. How did it make them feel? Were they frightened or did they feel secure and warm inside their houses? Why is rain important? Explain that they are going to work together to become a thunderstorm.

In the Classroom

Ask students to stand in a semicircle in front of you. Explain that when you make eye contact with or point to individual students, they are to imitate your motion (the series of motions follows). Students should continue their motions until you make eye contact again and begin a new motion, which they will imitate. Continue the motion as you make eye contact with students in turn around the semicircle. Make eye contact with the first student and start the second motion; others will continue your first motion. The cycle creates a crescendo as more students join in making the sounds and motions.

1. Rub your hands together.
2. Snap your fingers.
3. Clap your hands in an irregular cadence.
4. Slap your hands on your legs.
5. Stomp your feet while you continue slapping your hands on your legs.
6. Quit stomping your feet but continue slapping your hands on your legs.
7. Clap your hands in an irregular cadence.
8. Snap your fingers.
9. Rub your hands together.
10. Stop rubbing hands together (remember students are not to stop until you make eye contact with them).

Curriculum Extensions

- Students research kinds of thunderstorms.
- Students write stories about thunderstorms they have experienced. Where? When? What happened?
- Students draw pictures of the various things that happen during a thunderstorm.
- Students pantomime a thunderstorm.

Checking for Understanding

- Students compare a real storm to the movements. What stage did each movement and sound represent?

Reflection Prompts

▶ When I slapped my knees and stomped my feet I . . .
▶ The part of the thunderstorm I liked best was . . .
▶ I think . . .

Magic of the Sun

Process Skills Used:

data collection, comparison, observation

Purpose:

To observe ways the sun transfers energy in the form of heat to Earth

National Science Standard

4E: The sun warms the land, air, and water. Things that give off light also give off heat.

Literature Entry Point

Marzollo, Jean. *Sun Song.*
ISBN: 0-15-272198-3

A song that describes how magical the sun really is. Animals and plants respond to the sun's changing light over the course of a day.

Grades
4 through 6

Duration
30 to 40 minutes

Materials
❑ watches
❑ containers with lids
❑ black and white construction paper
❑ tape
❑ thermometers
❑ pencil
❑ data sheet

Site
School yard on a sunny day

Intelligences Used
naturalist
mathematical-logical

Background

Virtually all life on Earth depends on sunlight as its ultimate source of energy. We use energy produced by the sun's rays for heat and warmth. You may have noticed that you are warmer when you wear dark clothing and stand in the sun than when you wear light clothing. In this lesson, students observe and record how the sun warms the land.

Before You Leave the Classroom

Review how the sun provides energy in the form of heat and light, and how very important it is for all life on Earth. You may want students to think about a recent sunny day and what it felt like to be in the sun, then share what they felt on that day. You may also have them reflect on getting into a car that has been sitting in the sun for a long time with all the windows up. Once everyone who wants to has shared, tell students they will be working in groups of three to four to perform a test to see which color of construction paper warms faster in sunlight. They will be working with thermometers so review how to read one. Review outdoor safety rules, as well.

In the Field

Give each group two thermometers; one watch; and two containers with lids that have a small opening for the thermometer, one covered with white paper and the other with black paper. You may place a few rocks or water in the bottom of the containers to keep them upright. Students predict which container will increase in temperature quicker and tell why they make that prediction. Once students have their materials set up, they place their containers in direct sunlight. They check the temperature every two minutes for fifteen to twenty minutes and record the temperatures on their data sheets. While they collect data, ask students to write down words that describe how it feels to be in the sunlight.

Back in the Classroom

Students share with the other groups what they discovered. Which container's temperature increased faster? Why? Next, discuss ways that what they learned applies to clothing. Discuss the qualities of the sun and why it is important.

Curriculum Extensions

- Students create line graphs (time vs. temperature) for each container.
- Students write creative stories about all the things they can do on a sunny day.

Checking for Understanding

- Using different shades of construction paper, clothes, or painted pie tins, students predict which color's temperature will rise fastest and why. They conduct the experiment they used with the containers to see if their predictions are correct.

Reflection Prompts

- ▶ I now know that if I am wearing a dark color in the sun . . .
- ▶ My favorite part of this lesson was . . .
- ▶ I feel the sun is important because . . .

The Magic of the Sun Data Sheet

Name: _____

Prediction:

Time	Black Container Temperature	White Container Temperature
Starting (0 minute)		
2 minutes		
4 minutes		
6 minutes		
8 minutes		
10 minutes		
12 minutes		
14 minutes		
16 minutes		
18 minutes		
20 minutes		
Total Temperature Change = (Subtract final temperature from beginning temperature)		

3
Prediction

Forming an idea of an expected result based on inferences; guessing an outcome based on our experience or evidence.

Perceptions of the environment gained from [field and laboratory] experiences are the criteria against which we judge the appropriateness of our mental patterning.

—Jean-Michel Cousteau

I learned that we can't use the land just any way we want. It will take away the animals' homes and may cause them to become extinct.

—Student

Eagles and Salmon

Grades
1 through 6

Duration
45 minutes

Materials
❏ data sheet
❏ clipboard

Site
Outside or school gym

Intelligences Used
naturalist
bodily-kinesthetic

Process Skills Used:

prediction, data collection, analysis

Purpose:

To understand the concept of predator and prey; to "become" the eagle and experience the effect of a diminished food supply on living things within a habitat

National Science Standard

5D: Animals eat plants or other animals for food.

Literature Entry Point

Cone, Molly. *Come Back, Salmon.*
ISBN: 0-87156-572-2

This book chronicles the restoration of a salmon-bearing creek by an elementary school in Everett, Washington.

Background

Students should be familiar with the food chain and ways one thing in nature depends on others. All animals must eat other plants or animals to survive. Low food supplies on your school ground could limit species, including those native to the area. Some animals eat a great variety of foods while others eat one or two kinds. The diets of most animals change with the seasons as certain foods become available. When something causes a disruption in the food chain, many other living things feel the results. If a food source is eliminated, some animals may find it difficult to survive. A predator is an animal that hunts other animals. The prey is the hunted animal. To keep a healthy balance, adequate numbers of predators and prey must exist. Remind students that this simulation is not only a game. They should have fun but understand that they are "becoming" the eagles and the salmon to understand the roles of predator and prey.

Before the Activity

On the playground or in the gym, set up one-hundred-foot boundary lines about forty feet apart (see diagram). Students count off by four. The ones, twos, and threes are salmon. The fours are eagles.

In the Field

On the data sheet record under "round 1," students record the number of salmon and of eagles counted off. Eagles stand in the center of the area marked by the boundaries (see diagram). Salmon line up along one line. Signal the salmon in some agreed-upon way. Salmon swim to the other side and back, trying not to be tagged (eaten) by an eagle. Eagles may eat up to three salmon each in each round. Eagles who do not tag at least one salmon in the first round must sit in the designated area (see diagram) because they have starved to death. Tagged salmon sit in the designated area unless they are returned to the food chain in round 2. Some salmon will make it back safely. Students fill in the rest of the data sheet under "round 1."

In the appropriate area of the data sheet under "round 2," students predict what will happen to the numbers of salmon and eagles based on what happened in round 1. When you give the signal, pairs of salmon (students must hold hands) try to take one salmon from the area of eaten salmon (all three must hold hands, swim back to the opposite boundary, then back to start). They will not survive and reproduce if even one of the group is tagged by an eagle, so they must be very careful. The balance between predator and prey will alter in this step. After this round, students fill in their data sheets and discuss how the numbers changed. Why do students think the numbers changed in this way?

Eagles and Salmon Diagram

Area for eagles that caught no salmon

Eagles

Area for caught salmon

◄ Start line—Salmon ◄

All students participate in round 3. Explain that there has been an oil spill that has killed large numbers of salmon. Students count off by threes. Ones and twos are eagles and threes are salmon. The predators outnumber the prey. On the data sheet under "round 3," students record numbers and write their predictions of the number of salmon and eagles that will survive. At the signal, the salmon will swim across the field to the boundary line and back again. When this round is over, students fill in the remaining parts of the data sheet.

Back in the Classroom

Discuss the simulation with the students. What were they simulating when two salmon held hands and tried to release a fish to join their group? (reproduction) Why was it hard for the three salmon to swim around? (Salmon don't have ideal river conditions for spawning.) What happens to other things besides salmon when their number diminishes? Which round of the game was the most fun? Why?

Curriculum Extensions

- Students create a cartoon strip of a conversation between a salmon and an eagle.
- Students write a newspaper article that answers who, what, where, when, and why about the endangered population.

Checking for Understanding

- Students create simulations that involve other predators and prey.
- Assign a creative writing that requires students to predict what loss of a given habitat will do to the balance of predators and prey.

Reflection Prompts

- ▶ Today we . . .
- ▶ I understand how important . . .
- ▶ I think . . .
- ▶ I could . . .

Eagles and Salmon Data Sheet

Name: _____

Round 1

Beginning number of salmon	Number of salmon surviving after round 1

Beginning number of eagles	Number of eagles surviving after round 1

Round 2

Number of salmon I predict will survive round 2	Number of salmon that survive round 2

Number of eagles I predict will survive round 2	Number of eagles that survive round 2

Round 3

Number of salmon	Number of salmon I predict will survive round 3	Number of salmon that survive round 3

Number of eagles	Number of eagles I predict will survive round 3	Number of eagles that survive round 3

What do you think happens when there are more predators than prey?

_____

What other animals besides eagles rely on salmon for food?

_____

Why are salmon an important part of nature's balance?

_____

Discovering the Naturalist Intelligence, ©1999 Zephyr Press, Tucson, Arizona

Recycled Pumpkins

Process Skills Used:

prediction, data collection, observation, measurement

Purpose:

To understand decomposition and variables that affect it

National Science Standard

5E: Flow of matter and energy: Over Earth, organisms grow, produce new organisms, die, decay.

Literature Entry Point

Kroll, Steven. *The Biggest Pumpkin Ever.*
ISBN: 0-590-4113-6

This story is about two mice who have adventures as they grow a large pumpkin for a variety of purposes.

Background

Decomposition is the breaking down of once living materials into smaller parts. Bacteria and fungi break down dead organisms to use the nutrients for food. When decomposition takes place, certain chemicals are released as waste products. Some of these chemicals are raw materials that growing plants use to build new cells and tissues. Almost all decomposers need moisture, warmth, and oxygen. Imagine what Earth would be like if waste materials were not broken down in such a manner. Scientists estimate that the layer of dead organisms would be twelve miles deep.

Grades
4 through 6

Duration
1 hour

Materials
- ❏ tape measure
- ❏ shovels
- ❏ pumpkins
- ❏ paper bag
- ❏ plastic bag

Site
Field, flower bed, woods or other area that will not be plowed or dug up for several months

Intelligences Used
naturalist
bodily-kinesthetic
interpersonal
intrapersonal
mathematical-logical
verbal-linguistic
visual-spatial

Before You Leave the Classroom

Get one pumpkin for every two students. Local grocery stores or farms many times will donate distressed pumpkins for school projects. Students will study pumpkin decomposition using four methods: no burial, burial, burial with plastic cover, and burial with paper cover. Pair students and determine which method each pair will use. Students discuss and predict how their assigned methods will affect the rate of decomposition. What other factors will affect the rate? (pumpkin size, temperature, dampness of soil, types of soil organisms, holes or dents in the skin of the pumpkins).

Students inspect their pumpkins. They draw them, note the number of ridges and other identifying marks, and measure the circumference. Students might weigh the pumpkins. They record all information on their data sheets. Students predict how their pumpkins will change based on all factors. You might videotape students with their pumpkins before and after this experiment, which makes a nice visual and auditory record.

In the Field

Find a secluded place. Set up a grid with two measuring tapes set at right angles. Students measure from the edges of the measuring tapes with metric sticks to find and record a location to bury their pumpkins. Pairs with pumpkins that will not be buried will place them in tall grasses, bushes, or leaves, or find another way to hide them. The other groups add the assigned cover, if there is one, and bury their pumpkins in holes, covering them with at least four inches of dirt.

Back in the Classroom

As a class, students create a map of the area in which they buried their pumpkins. Flip charts with graph paper work well. Each pair marks the location of their pumpkin. Students make individual maps that show the locations of all the pumpkins.

Back in the Field

At selected intervals (two, four, and six months work well), students locate and unearth their pumpkins. They observe their pumpkins and record their observations, noting changes in color, texture, shape, smell, and so on. They look especially for evidence of decomposition, such as mold. Students may find it difficult to weigh pumpkins that have turned into amorphous, slimy masses. If you have a looping class, you might leave the pumpkins for a year. The longer the period of time the pumpkins are in the ground, the more decomposed they will be. In the cold north, not much decomposition will take place during the winter months. You might use a local greenhouse and buckets of dirt. In the warm, humid south or Hawaiian Islands, decomposition takes place very fast. Change the time frame according to your climate.

Curriculum Extensions

- Students measure various dimensions of the pumpkin: circumference, stem scar, thickness of walls, number of seeds, and so on.
- Students use the pumpkin as a globe and draw the world, complete with equator, longitude, latitude, North Pole, and South Pole.

Checking for Understanding

- On note cards, write the following situations. Students respond to each individually or work in groups on individual questions.

    1. Sally was eating lunch on the playground. She decided she didn't care for her bruised apple, so she threw it over the fence into the wooded area behind the school. Describe what will happen to the apple over time.

    2. Jose was eating his lunch from home and didn't have time to eat his peanut butter and jelly sandwich before recess. He left it in the plastic bag and threw it in the garbage. Describe what will happen to his sandwich over time.

    3. Fido is the neighbor's dog. He raided your garage and got into the ten pounds of potatoes. He pranced home and buried one potato with his favorite bone in the backyard. Describe what will happen to the potato over time.

4. Ruffy is the dog down the block. He wandered into your garage on a summer day and helped himself to a small brown bag full of onions. He buried them, bag and all, in your front yard. Describe what will happen to the bag of onions over time.

Reflection Prompts

▶ I liked this activity because . . .

▶ I did not understand this part of the activity:

▶ I would change the activity in this way:

▶ I thought the most difficult part of mapping the area was . . .

▶ I think it is like this underground:

▶ The following words describe how I felt when we buried the pumpkins:

▶ I like working with . . .

Recycled Pumpkins Data Sheet

Name: _____

	Type of Pumpkin and Burial Procedure
Starting Observations (attach sketch)	
Predictions	
First Observation	
Second Observation	
Final Observation	

Discovering the Naturalist Intelligence, ©1999 Zephyr Press, Tucson, Arizona

School Trek Survey

Process Skills Used:
prediction, observation, data collection, analysis

Purpose:
To observe the environment on a bus ride for one day, then predict what they will see the next day.

National Science Standard
2C: Numbers and shapes and operations performed on them describe and predict things about the world around us

Literature Entry Point
Trip Tracker: Travel Journal and Gamebook.
ISBN: 0-528-83843-1
This travel journal and game book has mapping and log activities plus a few observation sheets. It is designed to keep kids busy and happy on car trips and also to have them observe and learn.

Grades
3 through 6

Duration
Bus or car ride, or walk to and from school

Materials
❑ survey forms
❑ pencil

Site
community

Intelligences Used
naturalist
visual-spatial
verbal-linguistic
logical-mathematical

Background
This lesson gives students the experience of focusing and observing things they usually take for granted on the trip to and from school. By gathering data from the observations, students predict what they will see the following days. If students travel by car or bus, they must focus their observation skills to collect the data rapidly. Stress that students must manage themselves well to observe effectively under the conditions of a bus or car ride. All students begin their observations on the way home from school on the day you begin so the directions are fresh. They can then complete their survey on the trip to school the next day.

Before You Leave the Classroom
Go over the data sheet so everyone understands what they are supposed to find and record. Some sections of the sheet have been left blank for you or your students to fill in. You might consider the number of birds, road kills, family gardens, public playgrounds, stenciled storm drains, churches, or abandoned cars. Students make their predictions before they begin the survey. Instruct them to make a tally mark for each item as they see it; on the fifth item, they cross the previous four out, like this:

In the Field
Students observe and collect data listed on the data sheet on the way home. They count again to double check their numbers on the way to school the next day.

Back in the Classroom

Students tally the marks for each item. What differences do they find between their predictions and the actual numbers? They write that number in the last column on the data sheet, then graph the results for each item on the bar graph (page 76).

Group students who take the same buses together, the students who walked home together, and the students who took a car home together. Members of each group compare their results. Did all students in the group come up with the same numbers? If not, why not? (They might have sat in different areas of the bus, boarded and got off at different times, took various routes home, and so on). Was the observation difficult? Why or why not?

Students work together to make a class graph of all their results, the class school trek survey graph. What items occurred most? What surprised them about the results?

Students repeat the survey, first making predictions as before. Are their predictions different this time? Why or why not? What conditions might they be aware of this time that they didn't consider the first time (where they sit, the route they take, and so on)? They graph all results again and compare the results to the first set of data.

Curriculum Extensions

- Students graph the class average of data collected.
- Students list things they would like to see going to and from school.
- Students invent the ideal school community.
- Students draw pictures that represent the neighborhood.
- Students brainstorm problems and select one that the survey made evident. They plan and carry out a solution.

Checking for Understanding

- Students design a map of the trek to and from school. They create and use symbols for each item on the data sheet, placing the items appropriately.
- Students check the results of the second survey against their predictions. Were they more accurate than the first time?

Reflection Prompts

▶ I was surprised to see . . .
▶ Writing down observations was . . .
▶ I think we should . . .

School Trek Survey Data Sheet

Name: _____

Objects	Prediction Round Trip	Actual Count Way Home	Way to School	Total	Difference
stop signs					
people walking					
dogs					
cars with driver only					
fire hydrants					

School Trek Survey Data Sheet

Name: _____

Bar Graph Title (Individual or Class): _____

Method of transportation (bus, car, walking) _____

Bus number (if applicable) _____

34												
32												
30												
28												
26												
24												
22												
20												
18												
16												
14												
12												
10												
8												
6												
4												
2												
0												

stop signs   people walking   dogs   cars with driver only   fire hydrants

Discovering the Naturalist Intelligence, ©1999 Zephyr Press, Tucson, Arizona

Seed Gaiters

Process Skills Used:

prediction, observation, communication, categorization

Purpose:

To learn how seeds travel and grow into plants

National Science Standard

5D **Interdependence of Life:**

Organisms interact with one another in various ways besides providing food. Many plants depend on animals to transport pollen to other plants or to disperse seeds.

Literature Entry Point

Jordan, Helene. *How a Seed Grows.*
ISBN: 0-06-445107-0

This easy-to-understand story takes the reader from the development of seeds to how they are dispersed to the actual growth. Includes suggested activities.

Background

Many plants reproduce by producing seeds. These seeds have various amounts of food for the baby plant. Some seeds, such as a coconut, are huge; others, such as orchids and poppies, are very small. Some seeds are inside pods, nut shells, or fruits. Various seeds spread to new areas in various ways. The wind carries some, water carries others, and animals carry still others in their digestive tracts or in their fur. The hitchhikers cling to passersby and ride to new locations. They use special hooks, burrs, or other attachments that work like Velcro. Students might be interested to know that George de Nestral took a good look at how seeds hung onto animal fur, then invented Velcro based on his findings.

Before You Leave the Classroom

The best time to try this activity is late summer or early fall when seeds have formed. Using your science book or another resource, brief students on seeds. Include size, contents (embryo, endosperm, and so on), growth patterns, and dispersal mechanisms of various local varieties. Students put on gaiters. The old socks can go on right over their shoes. If students use the flannel pieces, wrap the pieces around the legs between the knee and the ankle. Fasten them with rubber bands or Velcro. If you don't mind spending some money, try some fake fur.

In the Field

Students collect seeds in one of two ways—by observation and the seed collecting gaiters. Students with gaiters walk through unmown fields, meadows, vacant lots—any area that has

Grades
1 through 6

Duration
1 hour and 20 minutes

Materials
☐ note cards
☐ transparent tape
☐ plastic bags
☐ old big socks (the fuzzier the better), old dish towel–sized pieces of flannel sheets or pillow cases to use as gaiters

Site
Vacant lot with weeds, meadow, or forest understory with annual plants.

Intelligences Used
naturalist
bodily-kinesthetic

a lot of annual plants. Students "wade right in" to a weedy, grassy area. Other students work in pairs and canvas the area collecting seeds, berries, or fruits such as dandelions, maples, Canadian thistles, Queen Anne's lace, cockleburs, yarrow, teasel, or milkweed. Students don't need to know names of plants, but you might require them to sketch the parent plant on the note card and tape the seed on the card. Is the seed encased in a fruit, berry, or hard shell?

Back in the Classroom

Students carefully take off the gaiters and examine them for hitchhikers. The other students share the cards with their seed finds. Students predict how individual seeds are spread or dispersed based on size, texture, weight, color, shell, or nutritional value to animals. Place students in groups of three and give one seed simulation card to each group. The groups simulate the various ways seeds are dispersed by acting out the situations on their cards. The rest of the group guesses the process the performing group is simulating.

Curriculum Extensions

- Students look at seeds under a hand lens or microscope and sketch them. Many seeds have hooks, barbs, or spines. Some of them are as sharp as fishhooks and may even stick to fingers.
- Students experiment on the seeds to find out possible dispersal methods. Does the seed float in water? Is it blown by a fan or hair dryer? Does it stick to animal fur or socks? Will a gerbil or mouse eat it?
- Students design experiments to test the strength of various nut shells.
- Students collect seeds by placing petroleum jelly or strips of masking tape, sticky side out, on a sheet of cardboard. They attach the cardboard to stakes, place stakes in the ground in a field, and leave them overnight.
- In the bulk food section of your grocery store, buy sesame seeds, sunflower seeds, pumpkin seeds, popcorn, dry beans, peas—whatever catches your fancy. Students use the seeds to make collages.

Checking for Understanding

- Students design a seed (on paper or three dimensional) that has specific characteristics for survival and dispersal. They use a scenario from the simulation or one of the following scenarios to write the life story of their seed.
  - Bears eat fruits. They cannot digest the small seeds and pass them later in fecal matter.
  - Beans, peas, geraniums, and violets scatter their seeds with a toss.

Reflection Prompts

- ▶ I think seeds are important because . . .
- ▶ I learned that seeds can . . .
- ▶ I found the following kinds of seeds:
- ▶ I was not able to identify some of my seeds because . . .
- ▶ I would like to find . . .
- ▶ If I could be any seed I would like to be a _____ because . . .

Seed Gaiter Data Sheet

Name: _____

Name of seed (if known)	Drawing of seed	Predicted dispersal method	Actual dispersal method

Seed Simulation Cards

Name: _____

This seed is very light. It travels in on the wind in large groups. Examples: dandelion, milkweed

---

This seed is one of the largest of all seeds. It floats on the world's oceans to a new land mass where it germinates and grows. Example: coconut

---

This seed attaches itself to the fur of animals or the clothes of humans. Examples: burrweed, thistle

---

This seed is in berries. Birds eat it and carry it long distances before expelling it in their waste. Examples: blackberries, elderberries, strawberries

---

This seed is considered a nut. It is harvested by squirrels and chipmunks and stored for the winter. The squirrel usually forgets to uncover it and it grows into a new tree. Examples: firseed, hazelnuts

---

This seed is very tiny and thousands are scattered by the wind in tropical areas. Example: orchid

---

This seed is often called a helicopter. It travels on the wind by twirling around like the blades of a helicopter. Examples: maple, ash

---

Discovering the Naturalist Intelligence, ©1999 Zephyr Press, Tucson, Arizona

Sow Bug Senses

Process Skills Used:
prediction, observation, data collection

Purpose:
To learn a way to determine which habitat sow bugs prefer

National Science Standard

1C Scientific Enterprise:
A lot can be learned about plants and animals by observing them closely, but care must be taken to know the needs of living things and how to provide for them in the classroom. In doing science, it is often helpful to work with a team and to share findings with one another. All team members reach individual conclusions about what the findings mean.

Literature Entry Point

McDonald, Megan. *Insects Are My Life.*
ISBN: 0-531-07093-X

Amanda loves bugs. She is willing to combat family and peer pressure to influence friends and foes alike to defend insects.

Grades
4 through 6

Duration
60 minutes

Materials
- ❑ sow bugs
- ❑ black paper
- ❑ small, square, clear plastic container with lid
- ❑ paper towels or blotter paper
- ❑ food (potato, oatmeal, apple, cat food, raisins, leaves, dirt, compost, and so on)

Site
Under boards, rocks, flower pots; outside or inside depending on weather

Intelligences Used
naturalist
bodily-kinesthetic
interpersonal

Background

The sow bug is a small land animal about the size of your little fingernail. It is not an insect but an arthropod that is related to the lobster, shrimp, and crab, which are part of a class called *Crustacea.* The sow bug is an *isopod.* All arthropods have an outside skeleton made of tough materials called *chitin,* which covers their bodies, and have jointed appendages. Sow bugs have flat oval bodies and joints in their backs. They have nine body segments and seven pairs of legs. They also have a pair of antennae on their heads. One type, called a *pill bug,* rolls into a ball when disturbed. Regional names that you might hear for sow bugs are *grubs, wood-lice, wood-louse,* and *potato bugs.* Sow bugs will eat almost anything that is soft and moist—potatoes, wet oatmeal, and apples. Interestingly, they breathe through gills, so you must keep them in a moist environment.

So where are these guys? You can find sow bugs easily under boards, flower pots, wood piles, logs, leaf piles, compost piles, and other moist, dark, warm areas. Females collected in the fall will bear as many as two hundred young in February. They carry their eggs in a brood pouch on the underside and near the posterior. Baby sow bugs emerge looking like lighter, miniature sow bugs.

Before You Leave the Classroom

Tell students about sow bugs. Discuss their habitat requirements and get a place to keep them ready. Even humans would have a difficult time surviving without their clothes, homes, heat, and machines. Tell students where they can find sow bugs outside.

In the Field

Students collect sow bugs. They predict how many of six sow bugs will prefer the various types of environment: light or dark, dry or wet. Students tape black paper on the outside of one-half of the top and bottom of a plastic cookie box and put about six sow bugs in the box. They leave the box alone for three minutes, then open the box and note where the sow bugs have gathered. They repeat the experiment three times.

For the next experiment, students remove the dark paper. They place a dry paper towel in one half of the plastic box and a damp paper towel in the other half. They wait three minutes and record which side the majority of the sow bugs crawl to. They repeat the experiment three times.

Back in the Classroom

Develop a large class chart with the results of everyone's findings. List the sow bug's habitat requirements.

Curriculum Extensions

- Students find out some foods sow bugs like to eat. They try cat food, apples, oatmeal, potatoes, and others. Ensure they keep all factors other than food consistent.
- Students design an experiment in which they find out what temperature sow bugs prefer.
- Students find out about the natural predators of sow bugs.
- Students make a diorama of a sow bug habitat.

Checking for Understanding

- Students write and illustrate a story about a day in the life of a sow bug. They include all activities: breathing, resting, eating, growing, reproducing, and finding shelter. They compare a day in the life of a country sow bug and a city sow bug.
- Students put on a puppet show that illustrates what a sow bug needs to be happy and safe.
- Students write an essay about the life and times of sow bugs. They include the information they collected through their experiments.

Reflection Prompts

- ▶ I noticed the following about the sow bug's environment:
- ▶ I discovered that sow bugs . . .
- ▶ I felt this way when I found my sow bug . . .
- ▶ I think my sow bug likes to eat . . .
- ▶ I would like the diet of a sow bug because . . .
- ▶ The most interesting thing I learned about sow bugs was . . .
- ▶ I thought the best experiment was _____ because . . .

Sow Bug Senses Data Sheet

Name: _____

The Moisture Test

Instructions: Predict how many of six sow bugs will like wet conditions and how many will like dry conditions. Let's find out. Find at least six sow bugs. Place a dry paper towel over one-half of the bottom of the cookie container, and a damp paper towel over the other half. Place six sow bugs in the center of the container. Cover the cookie container and, without disturbing it in any way, wait three minutes. Open the container and count the number of sow bugs on each half. Repeat the experiment three times. Have fun!

	Predicted Number on Wet Towel	Predicted Number on Dry Towel	Actual Number on Wet Towel	Actual Number on Dry Towel	Other? Explain
Number of Bugs					
Number of Bugs					
Number of Bugs					
Total =					
Average (divide totals by 3) =					

Discovering the Naturalist Intelligence, ©1999 Zephyr Press, Tucson, Arizona

Sow Bug Senses Data Sheet

Name: _____

The Food Test

Instructions: Put one type of food in each corner of the cookie container. Place the group of sow bugs in the center and observe. Be careful not to disturb the bugs while you are observing.

	potato chips	Oreos	Gummy worms	dry oatmeal	potato	none
First 10 minutes						
Second 10 minutes						
Third 10 minutes						

I discovered that most sow bugs like to eat _____

How did you really know that the sow bugs were eating?

Sow Bug Senses Data Sheet

Name: _____

The Natural Environment Test

Instructions: Conduct the last experiment, placing the items in the chart in the various corners and the bugs in the center.

	Leaves	Dirt	Roots	Wood	Other Explain
First 10 Minutes					
Second 10 Minutes					
Third 10 Minutes					

Sow Bug Senses Data Sheet

Name: _____

The Light and Dark Test

Directions: Tape black paper over one-half of the cookie container and clear plastic wrap over the other half. Predict which half most sow bugs will go to. Place four to six sow bugs in the center of the container. Observe them for 2 to 3 minutes. Be careful not to disturb the bugs while you observe.

	Predicted Number on Light Side	Predicted Number on Dark Side	Actual Number on Light Side	Actual Number on Dark Side	Other? Explain
Number of Bugs					
Number of Bugs					
Number of Bugs					
Total =					
Average (divide totals by 3) =					

Why Mud Puddles?

Process Skills Used:

prediction, observation, analysis

Purpose:

To learn that soil acts as a filter and that soil characteristics will determine how fast water can move through

National Science Standard

11A: Thinking about systems means looking for how every part relates to others. The parts usually influence one another.

Literature Entry Point

Markle, Sandra. *A Rainy Day.*
ISBN: 0-531-05976-6

> *A little girl explores why rain comes, what rain does, and where rain goes.*

Fleischman, Sid. *McBroom's Wonderful One-Acre Farm.*
ISBN: 0-688-15595-2

> *Hilarious story about soil so rich that seeds spring up to full-grown plants within minutes.*

Background

Rocks immediately below Earth's surface hold more than 2 million cubic miles of water—about forty times that in all rivers, lakes, ponds, and marshes in the world. Water seeps through the ground's zone of aeration into pores in the rock. Below that level, water accumulates in the zone of saturation. The type of surface soil determines whether water runs off or soaks in. How fast water moves through soil (permeability) depends on several soil factors: grain size, space between grains, compaction, saturation, and rate of precipitation. Impermeable surfaces include blacktop, buildings, and city streets. Soils are best for plant growth if they are a combination of sand, silt, and clay so that water can move through, but not so easily that it takes soluble minerals away from the plants. Too little water can slow the breakdown of minerals that are the vital nutrient source for plant growth. How fast water moves through soil determines the soil's permeability, which depends on several factors (grain size, space between grains, the degree of compaction, the amount of water the soil already holds, and the rate at which the water drops on the soil). Large amounts of impervious surface in your school yard will cause quick saturation of the soil (soil can't hold any more water) and mud puddles will form after a storm.

Grades

5 through 6

Duration

90 minutes

Materials

- [ ] paper
- [ ] pencil
- [ ] clipboard
- [ ] 2- or 3-inch PVC pipe cut into 8-inch lengths, marked with black permanent marker 3 inches from bottom, all ends smoothed
- [ ] measuring cup
- [ ] water
- [ ] watch

Site

Area of school grounds where surface is exposed soil, such as heavily traveled paths and flower beds. Pea gravel and sandy soil such as in a sand box would provide test spots.

Intelligences Used

naturalist
bodily-kinesthetic
mathematical-logical

Before You Leave the Classroom

Review observation and mapping skills (including estimating by stride, landmarks). Demonstrate a way to collect soil using a cut-off clear plastic pop bottle with soil in it. Map out a study area in the school yard in which students will mark their sites and draw their samples.

In the Field

Students experiment to find out if water soaks into the soil faster in some areas in the school yard than in others. They follow the instructions on their data sheets and fill out the sheets.

Back in the Classroom

Record data from the class. Possible questions to discuss include the following: When would it be best to do this experiment—after a heavy period of rain or after a period of no rain? Were differences in soil apparent? Was the soil packed in some areas? Why? Did the water soak in at different rates in different areas? Which soils allowed water to soak in? Why would we want water to soak in? What happens if water does not soak in?

Curriculum Extensions

- Students do the experiment after a long dry spell and again after a rainy period; they compare the data.
- Students do tests in their yards at home.
- Students do the experiment at the beach, in the mountains, or in the desert and share their findings with the class.
- Students grow plants in each type of soil in the school yard. Be sure they keep all other conditions the same.
- Students note on a map where water is standing on school grounds.
- Students ask a city engineer to help them calculate the amount of impervious surfaces in the school yard and how much water is diverted as a result. Where does the water go?

Checking for Understanding

- Students brainstorm reasons for the soak-in times in the chart on page 89 by answering these questions: What has happened to the soil on the path? Why does it take the water so long to soak in on the path? What would a gardener or farmer do to the soil so it would soak in easier? Why might people poke holes in their lawns? Why did the soil in the flower bed soak up water so fast? Why did the gravel allow water to pass through so fast?

Reflection Prompts

- ▶ I liked doing this activity because . . .
- ▶ This is how I see the connection between rain and mud puddles:
- ▶ I am most like a rain storm in the following ways:
- ▶ I am least like a rain storm in the following ways:
- ▶ If I could change the soil in the school yard, I would . . .

Saturation Times

Condition	Time
Heavily traveled path between the front door and the play shed.	4 minutes
Flower bed next to the windows underneath the eaves.	2 minutes
Pea gravel area near the parking lot.	30 seconds
Long jump pit or sand box.	1 minute

Mud Puddles Map

Name: _____

Select four different sites within the study area and number them.

Draw a map in the space below and, measuring from a landmark, indicate exactly where your sites are located or use a copy of another map of the school yard.

Mud Puddles Data Sheet

Name: _____

At each site, gently twist your PVC section three inches into the soil (up to the mark).

Pour one cup of water into the top of the pipe.

Time how long it takes the water to soak in.

Record you findings in the chart.

Site	Description	Predicted Time	Actual Time
1			
2			
3			
4			

We All Live Downstream

Grades
3 through 6

Duration
Design could be a homework assignment. Allow plenty of time to be creative. Sharing of land use should take 1 to 2 minutes per child. Writing of paragraph and editing should take two periods.

Materials
❑ One section of river to design for each student
❑ crayons or markers
❑ paper
❑ pencils

Site
Classroom

Intelligences Used
naturalist
interpersonal
visual-spatial
verbal-linguistic

Process Skills Used:

prediction, communication

Purpose:

To understand ways humans affect land use and water quality along a river

National Science Standard

11B: A model of something is different from the real thing but can be used to learn something about the real thing. Seeing how a model works after changes are made to it suggests how the real thing would work if the same were done to it.

Literature Entry Point

Cherry, Lynne. *A River Ran Wild.*
ISBN: 0-15-200542-0

This beautiful picture book shows the negative impacts humans have on a river system over time and ways the quality of the river was restored through hard work and problem solving.

Background

A watershed is the land that water flows across or under on its way to a river, stream, lake, or ocean. Water soaks into the ground to form groundwater, or it drains to one spot (like to a bath tub drain) where it empties into a river, stream, or ocean. Large watersheds are composed of many smaller ones. Puget Sound is composed of many smaller watersheds such as the Nisqually River watershed and the Cedar River watershed. Point pollution is pollution whose source you can identify. (You can point to it.) Nonpoint pollution is pollution you can't identify. It is much harder to clean up or control.

In the Field

Students construct a large dirt pile on the playground or school grounds. Use a garden watering can and sprinkle water on the pile to simulate rain. Watch as the water either soaks into the pile (groundwater) or runs down and off the pile to the concrete (the dirt sheds the water).

Back in the Classroom

Randomly assign each student one of ten sections of a watershed near a river. Ask them to represent in a visual form how they would use this river front property if given one million dollars. They will choose something to represent the pollution their use of the land will cause. They write paragraphs that explain their decisions. The paragraphs will explain the ways in which their uses of the land will affect water quality and the quality of the water downstream. Lay the ten sections from the top of the watershed (mountains) to the bottom (mouth) on the floor of the classroom as students read their paragraphs and explain their visual representations of the pollution. Students pass the objects they chose to represent pollution to the next person in line as they speak. The person at the mouth ends up with everyone's pollution, which can lead to a discussion of point and nonpoint pollution and possible solutions to and ways to prevent pollution.

Curriculum Extensions

- Students find out who will know about land use rules and regulations related to water quality in your community. They research the rules and regulations.
- Students identify community experts (farmers, loggers, wildlife experts) and invite them to present information on land use management to the class. How do these people protect the river or other water from erosion, pesticides, and fertilizers?
- Students research things that can pollute water and research a water treatment plant.

Checking for Understanding

- Students give examples of point and nonpoint pollution.
- Students make a T-chart for their chosen use of land. In one column, they list the problems with their land use; in the other, suggestions for correcting or avoiding those problems.
- Everyone selects the section they would want to live in and lists the reasons.

Reflection Prompt

- ▶ People who live near a river need to . . .
- ▶ I think the best way to keep water clean is to . . .
- ▶ I can . . .
- ▶ I learned that water . . .

We All Live Downstream Data Sheet

Name: _____

Enlarge and reproduce each section on an 8½-inch-by-11-inch sheet of paper. Notice the Roman numerals so you can put them back in order. There will be ten full-page patterns, one for each student. If you have thirty students, you will need thirty patterns to have three watershed systems.

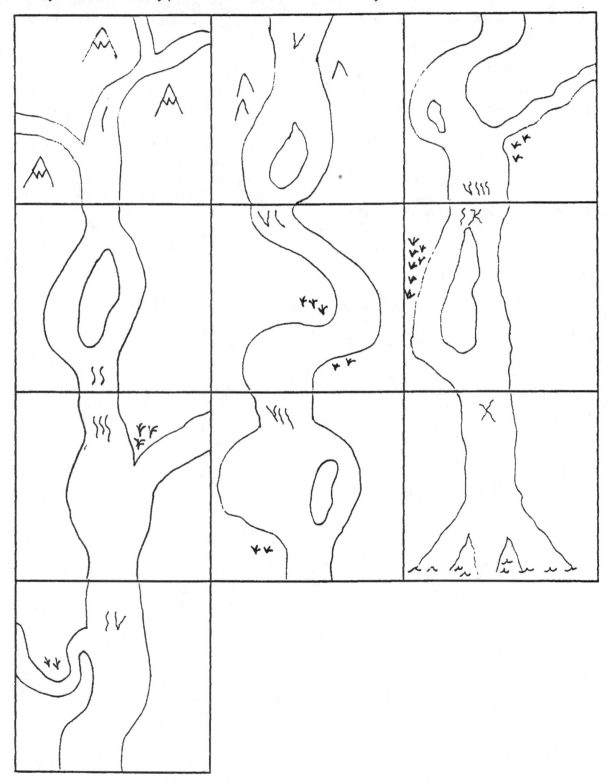

Discovering the Naturalist Intelligence, ©1999 Zephyr Press, Tucson, Arizona

4
Analysis

Looking at the data and trying to discover what it means

Nature has . . . some sort of arithmetical-geometrical coordinate system, because nature has all kinds of models. What we experience of nature is in models, and all of nature's models are beautiful.

—Buckminster Fuller

I learned a lot of things this year by going outside. One thing I learned was that over just a short time you can see a big difference in the way things in nature look.

—Student

Critter Creatures

Grades
1 through 6

Duration
30 minutes observation
and discussion; 45
minutes construction

Materials
- ❑ potatoes
- ❑ carrots
- ❑ paint
- ❑ toothpicks
- ❑ sticks
- ❑ pipe cleaners
- ❑ cardboard
- ❑ feathers
- ❑ cotton balls
- ❑ glue
- ❑ scissors
- ❑ anything else you may
     have in your closets
- ❑ creature cards

Site
Classroom or playground

Intelligences Used
naturalist
bodily-kinesthetic
visual-spatial

Process Skills Used:

analysis, observation, data collection

Purpose:

To create an animal that will survive in an assigned habitat

National Science Standard

5F: Different plants and animals have external features that help them thrive in different kinds of places.

Literature Entry Point

Brett, Jan. *Town Mouse, Country Mouse.*
ISBN: 0-399-22622-2

A town mouse and a country mouse trade habitats (homes). Their daily habits and comfort levels change as a result.

Background

All living things require homes to survive. A habitat is the place in which an animal or plant lives. That plant or animal species has adapted to that environment to allow it to grow and reproduce. The habitat includes food (seeds, berries, nuts, flower nectar, insects), water (ponds, puddles, streams, bird baths, drip faucets, sprinklers), cover (trees, shrubs, brush piles, rock piles, hollow logs, snags), and space (open space, wildlife corridors, green spaces). The size and health of a wildlife population are determined by the available resources within its habitat.

Before You Leave the Classroom

Discuss with the class some ways animals have adapted to help them survive. Include color, body structure, and certain sensory adaptations. Explain the purpose of this activity. Students will create an animal that can survive in their schoolroom or playground habitat. They will first select a critter creature card that lists the playground habitat, then observe the conditions (food, water, cover, space) that exist in that spot. Remind students what outdoor behavior you expect. Hand out or have them select a critter creature card.

In the Field

Students observe their individual habitats, taking notes on where water, food, cover, and space are located. They might also make observations of the entire area.

Back in the Classroom

Brainstorm a list of natural elements on the play-ground so students have additional knowledge and choices to pull from. Discuss colors and objects (trees, flowers, tall grasses, weeds, gravel, and so on). Students construct creatures in a way that ensures they will be safe in their habitats and have all the things they need. Students will include adaptations to the environments and give the creatures characteristics for protection and sur-vival. We have also included a set of classroom critter cards. If you select the classroom as a habitat, place students' completed crit-ters in the designated area of the room.

Curriculum Extensions

- Students write individual stories using their creatures as main characters.
- In teams of four, students arrange their creatures in a food chain. Each group presents and explains how the food chain works.
- Challenge students to design creatures that would survive in the desert, ocean, prairie or tundra.

Checking for Understanding

- Students present their creatures to the class, naming their creatures and describing the physical characteristics that help each adapt to its habitat.
- Students change one feature of the assigned habitat and explain how that would affect their creature's ability to survive. In what ways would the creature need to adapt to survive?

Reflection Prompts

- ▶ The best part about doing this lesson was . . .
- ▶ I think the habitat of an animal . . .
- ▶ I feel humans . . .

Critter Cards

Name: _____

Playground Habitat	Classroom Habitat
Create a critter that can live in the bark of a tree.	Create a critter that lives on the computer.
Create a critter that can live in a bush.	Create a critter that lives on the floor.
Create a critter that can live on a leaf.	Create a critter that lives on your desk.
Create a critter that can live in gravel.	Create a critter that lives in a dictionary on the bookshelf.
Create a critter that can survive in grass.	Create a critter that lives on the ceiling.
Create a critter that lives on the blacktop.	Create a critter that lives on the blackboard or whiteboard.
Create a critter that lives in a mud puddle.	Create a critter that lives in the recycle box.

Discovering the Naturalist Intelligence, ©1999 Zephyr Press, Tucson, Arizona

Cycle Bracelet

Process Skills Used:

analysis, communication

Purpose:

To create a model and tell the story of any natural cycle; to describe the elements of the model

National Science Standard

11B: Models are often used to think about processes that happen too slowly, too quickly, or on too small a scale to observe directly, too vast to be changed deliberately, or too potentially dangerous.

Literature Entry Point

Cannon, Janell. *Verdi.*
ISBN: 0-15-201-0289

Mom snake tells Verdi to grow up big and green. Verdi resists and has lots of adventures that demonstrate concepts of food chains and camouflage.

Grades
1 through 6

Duration
30 minutes construction;
30 minutes sharing

Materials
❑ various colored beads
❑ twine

Site
Classroom

Intelligences Used
naturalist
bodily-kinesthetic
visual-spatial
verbal-linguistic

Background

Cycles surround us. Birth, growth, and death is the cycle of plants and animals. The Moon goes through stages as it reflects light from the Sun. Earth moves from one season to another as it rotates and revolves around the Sun. The water cycle is one of the most important cycles in nature. The carbon cycle is another. Whenever we breathe in, we take oxygen out of the air. The body uses this oxygen to turn food into energy, producing carbon dioxide and water in the process. We then breathe out carbon dioxide, about two pounds every day. Trees and plants need carbon dioxide to live. Through needles or leaves, plants breathe in carbon dioxide. Through a process called *photosynthesis* plants turn that carbon dioxide into oxygen and breathe it out. A typical tree will consume twenty-five pounds of carbon dioxide a year. The person who has a strong naturalist intelligence sees the cycles in living things. Most students need experiences that simulate and explain connections among all things.

In the Classroom

Brainstorm words that relate to the water cycle or any cycle you are studying, for example, *evaporation, vapor, clouds, surface runoff, transpiration, condensation, precipitation, ground water,* and *percolation.* Students use colored beads to represent the cycle, making a bracelet of the steps. They retell the story they've composed on their bracelets, discussing what each color represents and the role it plays in the cycle.

Curriculum Extensions

- Other cycles you might have students represent include the life cycle of a plant or animal, human impacts on a watershed, and a food chain.
- Students act out the stories on their bracelets.
- Students construct a graphic organizer such as a flow chart to show sequence of and connections among events in nature.

Checking for Understanding

- Students write a paragraph or make a list that explains the relationship of the colors to the parts of the cycle.
- Students construct legends in which they interpret the colors of their bracelets.

Reflection Prompts

- ► The part of the cycle that was the hardest to find a color for was . . .
- ► I could change the order of the beads on my bracelet if . . .
- ► I feel it is important to . . .

Dead or Alive?

Process Skills Used:

analysis, classification, comparison, observation

Purpose:

To observe and classify objects in the school yard as dead or alive by applying criteria

National Science Standard

5C: Most living things need water, food, and air. Some living things consist of a single cell. Like other organisms, they need food, water, and air; a way to dispose of waste; and an environment in which to live.

Literature Entry Point

Emorg, Jerry. *Dirty, Rotten, Dead?*
ISBN: 0-15-200695-8

A worm's-eye view of death, decomposition, and life.

Grades
4 through 6

Duration
40 minutes

Materials
❑ data sheet
❑ pencil
❑ clipboard (optional)
❑ magnifying lens (optional)

Site
Any place in the school yard

Intelligences Used
naturalist
interpersonal
mathematical-logical
verbal-linguistic
visual-spatial

Background

Living things share five basic characteristics: they grow, reproduce, respond, have cells, and need food for energy. In order for something to be considered living, it must have all characteristics. Some things might have died, for example, leaves, birds, bugs, or "road kill." Other things have never been alive, such as rocks, sand, concrete, glass. Note: You may encounter some things that are a mixture of living and dead things, such as dirt. It is made up of a combination of small living things and eroded pieces of rock. It's your call; you decide whether you will accept such things as alive or dead.

Before You Leave the Classroom

Discuss with students the differences between living and dead. Students will work in pairs to write down names or descriptions of objects they see in the school yard. They take their information and classify the objects as dead or alive. Remember to review outdoor safety rules.

In the Field

Challenge students to observe, write names or descriptions, and classify as many things as they can. Encourage them to look up in trees, on buildings, down on the ground, and in grass and cracks.

Back in the Classroom

Give students time to review their data. They then list reasons for classifying the various objects as dead or alive. All students record their lists onto one master list on poster paper, the board, or an overhead transparency. As a class, discuss the findings, especially any discrepancies.

Curriculum Extensions

- Students create individual songs that tell the differences between those things that are alive and those that are dead.
- Students create mobiles or collages of items that represent the five characteristics of life.
- Students create bar or pie graphs that compare the number of alive objects to the number of dead objects.

Checking for Understanding:

- List several things that are alive (for example, tree, mouse, flower). Students give at least three reasons that each item is classified as alive.
- List several things that are dead (for example, rock, television, road). Students give at least three reasons that each item is classified as dead.

Reflection Prompts

- ▶ I know things are living because . . .
- ▶ I know things are dead because . . .
- ▶ What I really learned from this lesson is . . .

Dead or Alive Data Sheet

Name: _____

Instructions: Record objects you see in the school yard, then mark the box dead or alive for each. Tell why you know each object is dead or alive.

Object Name, Description, or Drawing	Dead?	Alive?	Why?

Discovering the Naturalist Intelligence, ©1999 Zephyr Press, Tucson, Arizona

Picture This

Process Skills Used:

analysis, comparison, data collection, observation, prediction

Purpose:

To analyze and predict change in a specified area over time using a photograph

National Science Standard

11BA: Model of something is different from the real thing but can be used to learn something about the real thing.

Literature Entry Point

Baker, Jeannie. *Window.*
ISBN: 0-14-054830

> *This book is about seeing changes that occur outside one window over the years.*

Background

This lesson presents a wonderful opportunity to introduce the concept of seasons. So many changes take place during seasons. How many can your students see during the course of the school year? Bill Nye's video *Seasons* covers the causes of the seasons and how the changes affect plants and animals.

Grades
4 through 6

Duration
Three 1-hour sessions

Materials
- ❏ camera
- ❏ tripod
- ❏ clipboard
- ❏ paper
- ❏ pencil
- ❏ individual laminated numbers
- ❏ map of school site

Site
Some site in the school yard that shows evidence of change between the seasons

Intelligences Used
naturalist
bodily-kinesthetic
intrapersonal
verbal-linguistic,
visual-spatial

In the Field

In the fall, students visit a site in the school yard that changes over the seasons. Each student uses a camera on a tripod to photograph a spot that has evidence of living things. The students attach their photographs to and record information on the data sheets. To ensure they can duplicate the same conditions, they measure the height of the tripod and record specific descriptive information about their site. Individual students record specific directions that will direct them to the same site later and place laminated numbers on their sites in the developed photograph. Students repeat the process at the same location in the winter and late spring, recording the new information on new data sheets.

Back in the Classroom

Students place their data sheets with the attached photographs in their field studies journals. After each trip, discuss and compare students' descriptions and conclusions. Students might also talk about their success in following their own directions back to the original spots. At the end of the year, reflect on and discuss the changes that are evident in the three photographs.

Curriculum Extensions

- Students make a to-scale map of the area.
- Students draw one object in the photograph.

Checking for Understanding

- Students discuss and review the data sheet.
- Students demonstrate their ability to find their spots using their maps.
- Using information from one picture, students predict what changes will be evident in the next picture.
- At the end of the year, students write reflections about changes at the site and what they learned from these changes.
- Individual students duplicate the procedure in a different site in the school yard.

Reflection Prompts

- ▶ The changes I noticed between fall and winter were . . .
- ▶ The changes I noticed between winter and spring were . . .
- ▶ The change that surprised me the most was . .
- ▶ From visits to the site, I have learned these things about seasons:

Picture This Data Sheet

Name: _____

Record the following data:

Trip number: _____

Date: _____ Time: _____

Temperature: _____

Weather conditions: _____

_____

_____

Height of tripod: _____

Obvious landmarks: _____

_____

_____

Laminated number of site: _____

Directions to spot where tripod was placed: _____

_____

_____

_____

_____

_____

Map, illustration, or photograph of spot:

Trash Trip

Process Skills:

analysis, observation, classification, prediction, data collection

Purpose:

To collect, identify, and sort trash from school property; to recognize intrinsic value of a litter-free environment; to draw attention to litter found in a school or community by using it in a collage or building trash monsters

National Science Standards

1C: Scientific Enterprise: In doing science, it is often helpful to work with a team and to share findings with others. All team members should reach their own individual conclusions, however, about what the findings mean.

8B: Discarded products contribute to the problem of waste disposal. Sometimes it is possible to use the materials in them to make new products, but materials differ widely in the case with which they can be recycled.

Grades
1 through 6

Duration
1 to 1 1/2 hours

Materials
❑ plastic gloves
❑ plastic garbage bags
❑ plastic tarp
❑ bathroom or nurse's scale
❑ tongs or chopsticks (optional)

Site
School grounds or road, parking lots, or nearby ditches

Intelligences Used
naturalist
bodily-kinesthetic
mathematical-logical

Literature Entry Point

Seltzer, Meyer. *Here Comes the Recycling Truck.*
ISBN: 0-9-85-335-5.

This true story tells a day in the life of female recycling truck drivers. Actual photographs document ways recyclable items are sorted and reprocessed.

Background

Litter is out-of-place garbage. It can be unsightly and unsanitary, and it can create problems for humans and other animals. Animals can become sick from eating it. Several studies reveal that many sea birds feed plastic pellets to their young; since there is no nutritional value in the pellets, the young starve. Animals also become entangled in some forms of litter. Some litter, such as paper and banana peels, is biodegradable. Some litter, such as glass, aluminum, and plastic, does not readily decompose and lasts a long time. Glass and pottery can last hundreds of years in water or soil. Plastic will eventually break down into smaller pieces, as evidenced on some beaches. The light, biodegradable plastic bags break down into plastic dust, which damages lungs. The answer is to reduce, reuse, and recycle, and put garbage in its place.

Before You Leave the Classroom

Review safety rules for handling litter. Use plastic gloves and tongs. Don't let students pick up anything such as dead animals, medical wastes, pill bottles or needles. List other materials that you think should be off limits. Be proactive and give students clear instructions. Place students into small teams. On a large map, divide the school yard into several sections.

In the Field

Each team picks up all the litter in their area during the designated time.

Back in the Classroom

Bring the trash back into the classroom or to a protected area. Put in on a tarp. In teams or as a class, group the trash into piles. Students decide the criteria for the groups. They predict the number of pieces or weight of each category, then count, order by size, and weigh the trash. Students use the collected trash for a collage or to build monsters.

Curriculum Extensions

- Invite a speaker from the local government to speak about the types of trash that can be recycled.
- Use the trash monsters or collage to start a schoolwide project against littering. One local group sculpted the trash collected along a stream into a salmon and mounted it on a board.
- Graph the numbers of each kind of trash.
- Find out who litters the school grounds (visitors, students, neighbors, wind, and so on).
- Research how long various types of trash last before decomposing.
- Get a large map of your town from the planning department, chamber of commerce, or somewhere else. Students use the telephone book to research places in your community where items can be recycled or reused and note these on a map. Places they might include are recycling stations for aluminum, glass, plastic, newspapers, cardboard, and so on; secondhand stores; used-book stores; used-record stores; and flea markets. Even old buildings are often taken apart and the material reused. Students compile their findings in a brochure. They might also get information for people who want to buy, sell, or donate items.
- Students put on a fashion show of recycled or reused bargains they found, or a skit of ways to reuse items.
- Groups develop learning centers that teach younger students how to reuse items in school projects.
- Students organize a schoolwide yard sale, conduct an antilitter campaign, or begin or expand on a recycling campaign at school.

Checking for Understanding

- Students write or draw a plan of ways to analyze the litter in a local park and a way to address or solve the problem.

Reflection Prompts

- ▶ The garbage I was most surprised to find was . . .
- ▶ I felt _____ when we were picking up garbage.
- ▶ I am already recycling the following:
- ▶ I would change my recycling by . . .
- ▶ I did not like _____ because . . .
- ▶ I had trouble understanding the following part:
- ▶ I would like to expand this project by doing . . .

5
Communication

Giving or exchanging information to discover answers

If you love it enough, anything will talk to you.

—George Washington Carver

We should keep using the outside as a place to be able to learn. We need to share what we learn with other people so they can understand how important it is.

—Student

...ary Hike

Process Skill Used:
communication

Purpose:

To imagine taking a hike through a wooded area to learn about connections in nature

National Science Standard

5E: Over Earth, organisms are growing, producing new organisms, dying, and decaying.

Literature Entry Point

Arnosky, Jim. *Walking in Wild Places.*
ISBN: 0-689-71753-9

This book discusses safety practices for hiking in the woods. It also points out things often overlooked by the hiker.

Grades
4 through 6

Duration
30 minutes

Materials
- ❑ tape or CD player
- ❑ appropriate music such as Enya's "Memory of Trees"

Site
A quiet place outside or inside where students can sit or recline comfortably

Intelligences Used
naturalist
visual-spatial
intrapersonal
verbal-linguistic

Background

Guided imagery provides a learning opportunity that all students, especially those with strong visual-spatial intelligence, need to experience. Take students on an imaginary hike before they go outside to experience the real thing, or take them on the hike with no outside follow-up. Guided imagery is much like listening to the radio before the invention of the TV. You may choose to do this activity indoors or outdoors. Outdoor smells, sounds, and fresh air might enhance the experience.

Before You Begin the Hike

Explain the purpose of this activity. Select appropriate background music to enhance the environment and improve the process. Review appropriate behavior. You may also need to write your own script to fit the environment around your school.

In the Field or the Classroom

Ask students to put away all items that might distract them. They will not talk during the hike. They sit in a comfortable position with their eyes closed and hidden, resting their heads in their arms, if possible. Allow the music to play for a period of time before you start reading the script. Read or speak slowly, calmly, and steadily, matching the background music. Continue playing the music for a while. Before students open their eyes, ask them to review all the images they saw. Ask them to open their eyes and discuss the experience. What image was the most vivid? If possible take the students on an actual hike.

Back from the Hike

With the class, discuss the experience and new information they learned. Did they see any connections between the imaginary hike and the real one?

Curriculum Extensions

- Students draw pictures of their favorite parts of the journey.
- Students use the hike as a setting to write a story.

Checking for Understanding

- Students write their own guided imagery scripts of a trip through nature (seashore, river rafting). Make sure they know to show connections.

Reflection Prompts

- ▶ Today I took a hike to . . .
- ▶ The most vivid image on the hike was . . .
- ▶ I think . . .
- ▶ I learned . . .
- ▶ I feel . . .

Hike through the Forest

It is a crisp fall morning. You approach the wooded area behind school. As you step onto the path and enter the woods, you immediately feel the air get cooler. The green shade of the towering trees soothes your eyes. With a few more steps, you leave the noise of the playground behind and the quiet stillness of the living forest surrounds you. The ground beneath your feet is soft with layers of fallen leaves and needles.

Off the trail the forest floor is covered with tall ferns and a carpet of moss. You bend down to touch the softness and see another soft part of the forest . . . a banana slug! This one is about six inches long and jet black. You watch it for a few minutes as it slides slowly along the ground on its own trail of slime, its two tentacles sensing the world around it.

Continuing along the trail, you are amazed at the height of the tall, skinny trees. They seem to sway in the wind like fancy toothpicks. There is one Douglas fir that is so thick you can't reach your arms all the way around its trunk. Its bark is rugged with deep ridges. You spot a bark beetle digging its way through the layers. You wonder how old this tree is—maybe 100, 200, 300 years or more?

There are other trees nearby: western hemlocks with lacy branches of short needles and lighter new growth; fresh green western red cedar with its distinctive stringy bark and drooping, scaly leaves. Suddenly you hear a noisy chattering coming from one of the higher branches and follow it until you see a bushy tail twitching back and forth. It is a squirrel, scolding you for intruding on its territory. It is holding a Douglas fir cone, pulling out the tasty seeds. Moving your eyes up the trunk, you try to find the very top of the tree; your neck hurts as you strain to see. The tree must be taller than most office buildings.

You move farther down the trail, with the squirrel's chattering as background music, and come upon a fallen log. It is as tall as you even though it has toppled over. Picking up a piece of the decaying wood, you feel the spongy texture and squeeze some water from it. On top of the log are several young hemlock trees growing, as well as moss and some mushrooms. These plants are getting a head start on life and taking needed nutrients and moisture from the large nurse log. Not far from the nurse log you see another dead tree that is still standing. The bark has fallen off, and you see oval holes halfway up the trunk. As you wonder who could have made the holes, you hear a loud hammering. The sound comes from a crow-sized woodpecker with a bright red chest. It ignores you as it hammers for wood-dwelling insects, then with sweeping wing beats flies off to another tree snag in search of more tidbits.

You walk down the narrow path to the lake behind the trees. The water is cold to the touch as you reach in through plants and tall grasses. You decide to sit and watch the water for a while. In the distance you can hear the cars buzzing down the road. You are very still and quiet. Out of the corner of your eye, you detect some movement at the water's edge. You slowly turn your head to see a small black-tailed deer drinking from the lake. Its ears are alert and its large dark eyes keep watch for possible danger. You barely breathe so as not to disturb it. It is so graceful. When it finishes drinking, it slowly, quietly strolls into the wooded area and disappears. You concentrate to listen to it moving through the brush. You hear nothing.

It is time for you to head back to class. You leave your spot and retrace your steps back to the narrow path and up the hill to the clear cut area. The sunlight filters through the trees. You notice the many different bushes, ferns, and other plants growing under the canopy of the trees. You feel relaxed and refreshed. You leave the woods knowing you can come back and explore another time. For centuries the forests have been home for many plants and animals and have provided food, water, shelter, and protection. You realize now that a forest is more than trees. Taking a deep breath, you walk out of the woods and over the playground's damp grass. You head back to the bustle of school.

Musical Message

Process Skill Used:
communication

Purpose:
To interpret patterns, rhythms, and lyrics in music as they relate to nature

National Science Standard
12D: Draw pictures that correctly portray at least some features of something being described.

Literature Entry Point
Crowdrey, Richard. *Animal Lullabies.*
ISBN: 0-06-024718-5
Incredible art work illustrates poems and lullabies. The sounds that surround animals are emphasized as they are lulled to sleep at night.

Background
Students can learn about nature through music, rhymes, and rhythms.

In the Classroom
Tell students to relax and to place their heads in their folded arms on their desktops. Play samples from the variety of nature tapes and ask students to identify the sounds. Then play the songs with lyrics. Students concentrate on the words and rhythm of the song and interpret what the writer is trying to say. Play the song again. Students visualize a story that the music shares. They draw the images of the stories. Continue to play the song as the students develop their pictures.

Curriculum Extensions
- Play instrumental music. Students draw pictures and write lyrics to the music.
- Students listen to a tape of bird calls. They invent a bird that matches the sound.

Checking for Understanding
- Students share pictures and stories.
- Students identify and replicate the rhythms and patterns that caused them to draw certain images.
- Students write stories to go with their illustrations.

Reflections Prompts
▶ The music made me listen for . . .
▶ I learned . . .
▶ I think music . . .

Grades
3 through 6

Duration
45 minutes

Materials
☐ crayons
☐ markers
☐ paper
☐ tape or CD player
☐ nature tapes (thunderstorms, rain forest sounds, and so on)
☐ music such as "Colors of the Wind" from the *Pocahontas* soundtrack and "Circle of Life" from the *Lion King* soundtrack or instrumental music

Site
Classroom or outside, if convenient

Intelligences Used
naturalist
musical-rhythmic
visual-spatial
intrapersonal

A Picture Is Worth a Thousand Words

Grades
1 through 6

Duration
30 to 40 minutes

Materials
❑ paper
❑ crayon
❑ pen or pencil
❑ clipboard or something
    else hard to write upon

Site
School yard or grounds

Intelligences Used
naturalist
visual-spatial
verbal-linguistic

Process Skills Used:

communication, comparison, observation, prediction

Purpose:

To orally communicate accurate descriptions of an object to a partner who draws the object

National Science Standard

12D: Draw pictures that correctly portray at least some features of something being described.

Literature Entry Point

Steptoe, John. *The Story of Jumping Mouse.*
ISBN: 068-801-902-1

The story of a mouse who loses his sight and smell and the many problems he faces as he tries to reach his dream land.

Background

Good communication and observations are very important in our world. Taking in information accurately is as important as sharing it in the same way.

Before You Leave the Classroom

Collect items from a designated area in the school yard for students to observe. As a class, practice describing the objects. Place students into pairs. Tell them their goal is to observe and describe objects so well that their partners will be able to draw the objects only from the description. Brainstorm good describing words. Next, review guidelines for appropriate outside behavior.

In the Field

Find a place in the school yard that allows students to sit comfortably and talk to each other without bothering other students. The artist has paper, a drawing utensil, and a hard surface. The describer chooses an object and observes it for a preapproved time. Partners sit back to back, with the describer's object still in view. The artist should not be able to see the object. Describers describe the object with as much detail as possible without saying what it is. Artists draw from the description. After five to ten minutes, drawers state what they think their individual objects are. Students compare their drawings with the actual objects. Students exchange roles.

Back in the Classroom

As a class, discuss the process. Give students time to reflect on the following questions: How accurate was your drawing? What words did you use to describe your item? What could you have changed to help the artist make the drawing more accurate? Why do you think it is important to describe things accurately? Why do you think it is important to take in others' observations accurately?

Curriculum Extensions

- Students write riddles, poems, or stories that describe objects in nature for others to guess.
- Individual students write a verse to a class song using the describing words they used for their objects.

Checking for Understanding

- Students write a clue card that used words to describe an object in the classroom. Collect the clue cards and read them aloud or pass out cards for students to draw.

Reflection Prompts

- ▶ The object that I chose to describe in the school yard was _____ . I chose it because . . .
- ▶ The most difficult part of describing objects to others is . . .
- ▶ The most difficult part about drawing from others' descriptions is . . .
- ▶ What I most enjoyed about this lesson was . . .

Riddle Me

Process Skills Used:

communication, observation

Purpose:

To use the senses in careful observation; to use a thesaurus to enliven and clarify descriptions

National Science Standard

1B: Scientific investigations may take many different forms, including observing what things are like. Describing things accurately is important in science because it enables people to compare their observations with those of others.

Literature Entry Point

Artell, Mike. *Wackiest Nature Riddles.*
ISBN: 0-80-69125-10

This book presents knowledge of nature facts in an enjoyable way and shows the importance of word choice in constructing riddles.

Background

The five senses are smelling, seeing, hearing, touching, and tasting.

Before You Leave the Classroom

Review the five senses with the students. Discuss ways they can use their senses to observe. Guide students in ways to use all their senses: smell and hearing (close eyes), sight (look up and down, not just out), taste (only with support from a knowledgeable adult). Mention that we rely on our sense of sight, but there are many other ways to collect data. Review appropriate outside behaviors and expectations. Go over purpose of lesson. Tell students that they will use the data to write riddles.

In the Field

Students choose any two objects and observe them carefully (with a hand lens, if available). Direct them to select fairly common, natural things. Objects can be rocks, pine needles, tree bark, or wildflowers. Students list at least one describing word for each category on the data sheet.

Back in the Classroom

Students use a thesaurus to find words to replace the common words they used on their data sheets. They compose two riddles to which the object is the answer. For example, "I am smallish, olive, lacy, delicate, and have very little odor. What am I?" (Lichen) They select their favorite of the pair to share with the class.

Grades
3 through 6

Duration
40 minutes

Materials
❑ data sheet
❑ pencil
❑ hand lens (optional)
❑ thesaurus

Site
Anywhere outside

Intelligences Used
naturalist
verbal-linguistic
interpersonal
mathematical-logical

Curriculum Extensions

- Students use their original descriptive words and the thesaurus words to construct a crossword puzzle.
- Students work in pairs. They exchange all the descriptive words and draw pictures of the object they think their partner's words describe.

Checking for Understanding

- Students list the page numbers in the thesaurus from which they got the words.
- Students copy paragraphs from their favorite nature books and underline common words. They rewrite the passages replacing the underlined words with words from the thesaurus. They read the passages to the class and discuss the differences and similarities.

Reflection Prompts

- ▶ Today I saw . . .
- ▶ I realize that . . .
- ▶ I learned . . .

Riddle Me Data Sheet

Name: _____

Object 1	Field Words	Thesaurus Words	Page
Size			
Color			
Shape			
Texture			
Odor			

I am _____, _____, _____, _____, _____, What am I?
          (size)   (color)   (shape)   (texture)   (smell)

Object 2	Field Words	Thesaurus Words	Page
Size			
Color			
Shape			
Texture			
Odor			

I am _____, _____, _____, _____, _____, What am I?
          (size)   (color)   (shape)   (texture)   (smell)

Discovering the Naturalist Intelligence, ©1999 Zephyr Press, Tucson, Arizona

A Vision in Nature

Process Skills Used:

communication, classification

Purpose:

To learn that various plants and animals live in various places called *habitats*

National Science Standard

5D: Living things are found almost everywhere in the world. There are different kinds in different places.

Literature Entry Point

Awan, Shaila. *The Burrow Book.*
ISBN: 0-399-21166-7

A book about all the imaginable animals that burrow into the ground

Background

A habitat is the location in which an organism lives. Many plants and animals share the same habitat. For example, in a tree, we might see moss, birds, and various bugs. In the soil, there are grasses, weeds, worms, and beetles.

Grades
1 through 6

Duration
45 to 60 minutes

Materials
- ❏ journal or paper for drawing or writing
- ❏ pencil

Site
Quiet place outdoors in which students can sit or lie down comfortably

Intelligences Used
naturalist
intrapersonal
musical-rhythmic
verbal-linguistic
visual-spatial

Before You Leave the Classroom

Tell students they will be doing an activity that will engage them in thinking about their thoughts (metacognition) and imagining that they are going on a journey through the environment outside the classroom. It is important that they do not talk during the activity. Your words will guide them through the journey. When it is over, students will share what their journey was like and how they felt.

In the Field

Take students to a comfortable and secluded spot, if possible. You can also do this activity in the classroom; however, it is more relevant if you do it in a natural setting. Give students time to settle in and relax. Follow the instructions on the activity sheet. Read slowly and improvise or pause to allow students to think or create the images in their minds.

Back in the Classroom

Give students time to process the experience. A good way to process is through drawing or writing in a journal. Ask students guiding questions, such as "What animals did you see and where did the animals live?" Take time to discuss the various plants and animals and the places they live. Discuss the various habitats that were mentioned as they were imaging.

Curriculum Extensions

- Students select various countries and research the plants and animals that live in the various habitats there.
- Students create scale maps or drawings of various habitats in the school yard.
- Students write poems that describe the various habitats in the community or school yard.

Checking for Understanding

- Students draw pictures, construct models, or write stories about their own habitats and the plants and animals that share them.

Reflection Prompts

- ▶ I felt the following things as I traveled down into the ground, then moved up the tree:
- ▶ What I learned from this experience is . . .
- ▶ What I will always remember from this lesson is . . .
- ▶ A habitat is . . .

A Vision in Nature

Close your eyes. Take a deep breath in, and let it out. Relax. (Pause) Focus on your breathing. Think of nothing but your lungs taking in air from the trees and plants around you. As you let it out, think about where that air goes. It travels slowly back to the plants that surround you. You provide a part of the food it needs for growth and those plants in return nurture you with the oxygen and air you breathe. Slowly breathe in, then out. In, then out. (Pause) Remember that you are connected to the plants around you.

As you lie or sit comfortably on Earth, think about the ways you are connected and touching Earth. (Pause) Take a moment to shrink your body until you are so small you can fit between the plants, the rocks, and tiny pieces of dirt. What lives below you? What small things live here? What do you see as you go deeper and deeper into the earth. (Pause)

As you make your way back to the surface, you pass by all your new friends. These little critters make all our grass clippings and leaves into the dirt that is home and food for plants.

Now you are floating up the side of a tree. Note what the tree looks like. (Pause.) Reach out and touch the bark, feeling it. Look up to see if your tree has

needles or leaves. Take a deep breath. (Pause) Notice the wonderful smells coming from your tree. Slowly move closer to the tree and look closely into the bark. See the little bugs wiggling under the cracks in the bark. You see a bird fly by your head. Notice what kind of bird it is. It begins to peck at the bark where the bugs live. It eats a few of them and flies off. You continue up the tree and notice beautiful patches of green soft stuff. You reach out and touch it. It is cool and moist. It is moss. You are now at a large branch of the tree. Examine the branch thoroughly. (Pause.)

Begin moving down the branch. A squirrel scurries by with a mouthful of cedar bark, on its way to make a nest for its family. You move farther down the branch and notice a tail. Look at the animal that is attached to this tail. Look down at the opossum with three little babies buried in its pouch. (Pause)

Wow! You realize that a lot of time has passed and it's time to get back. Move slowly to the ground, taking in a last glance at all the new things that you have discovered and how they are all connected.

Now, see and feel yourself lying on the ground. Focus on your breathing. In, then out. In, then out. Return to the smells of what surrounds you. (Pause) Feel the earth beneath you and slowly open your eyes; sit quietly and think about your journey. Think about what you saw and felt as you moved about. Look around you. Do you see any of those things now? (Pause) Look around as we walk quietly back to class.

Resources

Theory and Activities

Armstrong, T. 1994. *Multiple Intelligences in the Classroom*. Alexandria, Va.: ASCD.

Arnosky, Jim. 1993. *Crinkleroot's Guide to Walking in Wild Places*. New York: Alladin.

Castaldo, Nancy Fusco.1997. *The Little Hands Nature Book*. Charlotte, Vt.: Williamson.

Charles, Cheryl. 1992. *Project Wild*. 2d ed. Boulder, Colo.: Western Regional Environmental Education Council.

Cornell, Joseph. 1979. *Sharing Nature with Children: The Classic Parents' and Teacher's Nature Awareness Guidebook*. Nevada City, Calif.: Dawn.

Docekal, Eileen. 1989. *Nature Detective: How to Solve Outdoor Mysteries*. New York: Sterling.

FANDEX Family Field Guides. 1997. *Trees*. New York: Workman.

Gardner, Howard. 1983. *Frames of Mind*. New York: Basic.

———. 1991. *The Unschooled Mind*. New York: Basic.

———. 1993. *Multiple Intelligences: The Theory in Practice*. New York: Basic.

Hart, Diane. 1994. *Authentic Assessment: A Handbook for Educators*. Menlo Park, Calif.: Addison-Wesley.

Healy, Jane M. 1990. *Endangered Minds: Why Children Don't Think and What We Can Do About It*. New York: Simon and Schuster.

Higgins, Susan, Alan Kesselheim, Dennis Nelson, Sandra Robinson, and George Robinson. 1995. *Project WET*. Houston, Tex.: Western Regional Environmental Education Council.

Hogan, Kathleen. 1994. *Eco Inquiry*. Millbrook, N.Y.: Institute of Ecosystem Studies.

Lingelbach, Jenepher. 1986. *Hands-on Nature*. Woodstock, Vt.: Vermont Institute of Natural Science.

Mac's Field Guides series. 1994. Seattle, Wash.: Mountaineers.

McLuthan, T. C. 1971. *Touch the Earth*. New York: Outerbridge and Dienstfrey.

Mitchell, Andrew. 1989. *The Young Naturalist*. Tulsa, Okla.: EDC.

Mitchell, John Hanson. 1985. *A Field Guide to Your Own Back Yard*. New York: Norton.

Nabhan, Gary Paul, and Stephen Trimble. 1994. *The Geography of Childhood: Why Children Need Wild Places*. Boston: Beacon Press.

The New City School faculty. 1994. *Celebrating Multiple Intelligences: Teaching for Success*. St. Louis, Mo.: The New City School.

Ostlund, Karen. 1992. *Science Process Skills: Assessing Hands-on Student Performance*. New York: Addison-Wesley.

Perdue, Peggy K. 1991. *Schoolyard Science*. Glenview, Ill.: Scott, Foresman.

Pyle, Robert Michael. 1986. *Wintergreen: Listening to the Land's Heart*. Boston: Houghton Mifflin.

Roberts, Janet Wier, and Carole Huelbig. 1996. *City Kids and City Critters: Activities for Urban Explorers*. New York: Learning Triangle Press.

Rockwell, E. Sherwood, and R. Williams. 1986. *Hug a Tree and Other Things to Do Outdoors with Young Children*. Mt. Rainier, Md.: Gryphon House.

Roth, Charles, Cleti Cervoni, Thomas Wellnitz, and Elizabeth Arms. 1991. *Beyond the Classroom*. Lincoln, Mass.: Massachusetts Audubon Society.

Ruef, Kerry. 1992. *The Private Eye: Looking and Thinking by Analogy*. Seattle, Wash.: The Private Eye Project.

Shaffer, Carolyn, and Erica Fielder. 1987. *City Safaris: A Sierra Club Explorer's Guide to Urban Adventures for Grownups and Kids*. San Francisco: Sierra Club.

Share, Marjorie L. 1995. *Animal Tracks: Making Tracks to Care for Our Environment*. Washington, D.C.: A Conservation Education Program of the National Wildlife Federation.

Simon, Seymour. 1970. *Science in a Vacant Lot*. New York: Viking Press.

Simon, William L. 1985. *The Reader's Digest Children's Songbook*. New York: The Reader's Digest.

Sobel, David. 1998. *Mapmaking with Children*. Portsmouth, NH: Heinemann.

Swan, James A. 1992. *Nature as Teacher and Healer: How to Reawaken Your Connection with Nature*. New York: Villard.

Swan, Malcolm D. 1987. *Tips and Tricks in Outdoor Education*. Danville, Ill.: Interstate.

Tomera, Audrey N. 1989. *Understanding Basic Ecological Concepts*. Portland, Me.: J. Weston Walch.

Wilson, E. O. 1994 .*The Naturalist*. New York: Warner.

Additional Children's Literature

Arden, and Wall. 1990. *Wisdom Keepers*. Hillsboro, Ore.: Beyond Words.

Brett, Jan. 1994. *Town Mouse, Country Mouse*. New York: Putnam's.

Cannon, Janell. 1997. *Verdi*. San Diego: Harcourt, Brace.

Cole, Henry. 1995. *Jack's Garden*. New York: Mulberry.

Cole, Janna, and Bruce Degen. 1995. *The Magic School Bus Meets the Rot Squad: A Book about Decomposition*. New York: Scholastic.

Cooney, Barbara. 1985. *Miss Rumphius*. New York: Puffin.

Dorros, Arthur. 1987. *Ant Cities*. New York: HarperCollins.

Garelick, May. 1989. *Where Does the Butterfly Go When It Rains?* New York: Mondo.

Giesel, Theodor. 1997. *Seuss-isms*. New York: Random House.

Harvey, Gail. 1991. *Poems of Creatures Large and Small*. New York: Avenel.

Hickman, Pamela. 1991. *Bug Wise*. New York: Addison-Wesley.

Holzwarth, Werner, and Wolf Erlbrunch. 1994. *The Story of the Little Mole Who Went in Search of Whodunit*. New York: Stewart, Tabori, and Change.

Jeffers, Susan. 1991. *Brother Eagle, Sister Sky*. New York: Dial.

Jordan, Helene. 1992. *How a Seed Grows*. New York: HarperCollins.

Julivert, Angels. 1991. *Ants*. New York: Barrons.

Kneidel, Sally. 1994. *Pet Bugs*. New York: John Wily.

Lauber, Patricia. 1994. *Be a Friend to Trees*. New York: HarperCollins.

Locke, Thomas. 1995. *Sky Tree: Seeing Science through Art*. New York: HarperCollins.

Medlicott, Mary, and Ademola Akintola. 1995. *The River That Went to the Sky: Twelve Tales by African Storytellers*. New York: Kingfisher.

Moore, Lilian. 1995. *Poems Have Roots*. New York: Simon and Schuster.

Morgan, Sally. 1996. *Butterflies, Bugs, and Worms*. New York: Kingfisher.

Pelham, David, and Michael Foreman. 1995. *Worms Wiggle*. New York: Simon and Schuster.

Prelutsky, Jack. 1997. *Poems from the Animal Kingdom*. New York: Alfred A. Knopf.

Simon, Seymour. 1995. *Ride the Wind: Airborne Journeys of Animals and Migration*. San Diego: Browndeer Press.

Suzuki, David. 1991. *Looking at Plants*. London: John Wiley.

Thorson, Kristine, and Robert Thorson. 1998. *Stone Wall Secrets*. Gardiner: Tillbury House.

Young, Carolina. 1997. *The Big Bug Search*. London: Usborne.

Exercise All Their Intelligences with These Resources from Zephyr Press

SCIENCE THROUGH MULTIPLE INTELLIGENCES
Patterns That Inspire Inquiry
Robert Barkman, Ph.D.

Watch your students become confident, competent, and responsible investigators of the world around them when they use their multiple intelligences to interpret their environment. Each activity in *Science through Multiple Intelligences* is built upon an ecological principle, a scientific objective, and a national science standard. With each of the 36 outdoor lessons, you'll also have tasks, concepts, resources, and enrichment questions.

"Tap into student strengths with these brain-compatible teaching methods. The strength of the book is in the variety of guided inquiries that are suggested and the opportunities for taking each inquiry further."
—Anita Greenwood, Ed.D., Associate Professor, Science Education, University of Massachusetts

Grades 1–12
176 pages
ISBN: 1-56976-096-9
1093-W . . . $35.00

PATHWAYS OF LEARNING
Teaching Students and Parents about Multiple Intelligences
David Lazear
Foreword by Arthur L. Costa, Ed.D.

When you teach students about their multiple intelligences, you boost self-esteem, engage higher-order thinking, and make learning more interesting and fun. *Pathways of Learning* includes—

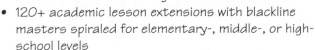

- 20 activities designed to encourage different levels of thinking and reflection
- 120+ academic lesson extensions with blackline masters spiraled for elementary-, middle-, or high-school levels
- Practical ways parents can nurture the development of intelligences in their children

Grades K–12+
288 pages
ISBN...1-56976-118-3
1115-W . . . $39.95

SCIENCE FOR EVERY LEARNER
Brain-Compatible Pathways to Scientific Literacy
Kathleen Carroll, M.Ed.

Link your teaching to national science standards and deepen your students' understanding of science through songs, stories, plays, experiments, journals, and portfolios. An outline will help you set teaching goals and ongoing assessments will keep your students on track. Lesson plans help you apply current learning theories to optimize learning for each student.

Grades K–8
208-page book and a 73-minute audiotape
ISBN: 1-56976-105-1
1105-W . . . $35.95

INVENTING TOYS
Kids Having Fun Learning Science
Ed Sobey, Ph.D.

Challenge your students to learn more through their own inventions while you monitor their progress in meeting benchmarks and National Science Education Standards. *Inventing Toys* makes it easy to teach through brilliant, tried-and-true creative problem-solving experiences and to tie inventing adventures to your science curriculum.

Grades 4–8
144 pages
ISBN: 1-56976-124-8
1121-2A . . . $23.00

Zephyr Press Offers the Best in MI Materials!
Choose from These Handy Resources

KID SMART
Posters for the Classroom
Created and illustrated by Donna Kunzler

Put up these bright posters so young students can learn to understand their strengths. Remind students how to use their multiple intelligences with easy-to-understand text and charming graphics. Includes the naturalist intelligence!

Grades PreK–6
9 full-color, 11" x 17" posters
ISBN: 1-56976-135-3
1815-W . . . $27.95

TAP YOUR MULTIPLE INTELLIGENCES
Posters for the Classroom
Text by David Lazear
Illustrations by Nancy Margulies, M.A.

Help your students learn about all eight intelligences with full-size color posters. Each poster reinforces a specific intelligence.

Grades 3–12
8 full-color, 11" x 17" posters
ISBN: 1-56976-134-5
1811-W . . . $27.95

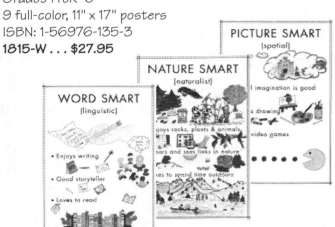

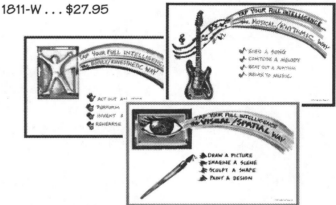

ORDER TODAY!

Qty.	Item #	Title	Unit Price	Total
	1093-W	Science through Multiple Intelligences	$35.00	
	1115-W	Pathways of Learning	$39.95	
	1105-W	Science for Every Learner	$35.95	
	1121-2A	Inventing Toys	$23.00	
	1815-W	Kid Smart Posters	$27.95	
	1811-W	Tap Your Multiple Intelligences Posters	$27.95	

Subtotal	
Sales Tax (AZ residents, 5.6%)	
S & H (10% of subtotal–min $5.50)	
Total (U.S. Funds only)	

CANADA: add 30% for S & H and G.S.T.

Name _____
Address _____
City _____
State _____ Zip _____
Phone (_____) _____
E-mail _____

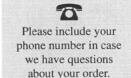

Please include your phone number in case we have questions about your order.

Method of payment (check one):
❏ Check or Money Order ❏ Visa
❏ MasterCard ❏ Purchase Order Attached
Credit Card No. _____
Expires _____
Signature _____

To order write or call
P.O. Box 66006-W
Tucson, AZ 85728-6006
800-232-2187 or 520-322-5090
Fax 520-323-9402
www.zephyrpress.com
www.i-home-school.com

Zephyr Press

About the Authors

Jenna Glock teaches biology and integrated science at North Thurston High School in Lacey, Washington. She has written integrated science and environmental curriculum for Washington State's EPA and Superintendent of Public Instruction, and has experience in using multiple intelligences in designing and implementing curriculum. Jenna is an active member of Global Rivers Environmental Education Network (GREEN). She received her master of education degree in technology from City University in Tacoma in 1996.

Susan Wertz has been a science teacher at the middle and high school level for more than 25 years. During this time, she has taken students outside to study lawns, parking lots, retention ponds, woods, and streams in her area. She serves as a community link coordinator, helping students make the transition between school and careers at the innovative New Century High School. Susan embraces multiple intelligences as a strategy for helping all students learn. She has been an active member of GREEN and the National Aquatic Marine Educators Association. She received a master of arts degree in science education from Central Washington University in 1975.

Maggie Meyer has been an elementary teacher for 26 years and is also a national trainer and facilitator for GREEN and Learning Environments Affecting the Future (LEAF). She has written many articles on a variety of issues, including some in *Educational Leadership.* She has extensive training and experience in using multiple intelligences to design and implement curriculum. As part of GREEN, she has developed an integrated water quality education program that meets national science standards. Maggie received a master of arts degree in curriculum design and instruction from City University in 1994.